THE PRINCETON REVIEW

Biology
Smart

BOOKS IN THE PRINCETON REVIEW SERIES

Cracking the ACT
Cracking the ACT with Sample Tests on CD-ROM
Cracking the CLEP (College-Level Examination Program)
Cracking the GED
Cracking the GMAT
Cracking the GMAT with Sample Tests on Computer Disk
Cracking the GRE
Cracking the GRE with Sample Tests on Computer Disk
Cracking the GRE Biology Subject Test
Cracking the GRE Literature in English Subject Test
Cracking the GRE Psychology Subject Test
Cracking the LSAT
Cracking the LSAT with Sample Tests on Computer Disk
Cracking the LSAT with Sample Tests on CD-ROM
Cracking the MAT (Miller Analogies Test)
Cracking the SAT and PSAT
Cracking the SAT and PSAT with Sample Tests on Computer Disk
Cracking the SAT and PSAT with Sample Tests on CD-ROM
Cracking the SAT II: Biology Subject Test
Cracking the SAT II: Chemistry Subject Test
Cracking the SAT II: English Subject Tests
Cracking the SAT II: French Subject Test
Cracking the SAT II: History Subject Tests
Cracking the SAT II: Math Subject Tests
Cracking the SAT II: Physics Subject Test
Cracking the SAT II: Spanish Subject Test
Cracking the TOEFL with Audiocassette
Flowers & Silver MCAT
Flowers Annotated MCAT
Flowers Annotated MCATs with Sample Tests on Computer Disk
Flowers Annotated MCATs with Sample Tests on CD-ROM

Culturescope Grade School Edition
Culturescope High School Edition
Culturescope College Edition

SAT Math Workout
SAT Verbal Workout

All U Can Eat
Don't Be a Chump!
How to Survive Without Your Parents' Money
Speak Now!
Trashproof Resumes

Biology Smart
Grammar Smart
Math Smart
Reading Smart
Study Smart
Word Smart: Building an Educated Vocabulary
Word Smart II: How to Build a More Educated Vocabulary
Word Smart Executive
Word Smart Genius
Writing Smart

Grammar Smart Junior
Math Smart Junior
Word Smart Junior
Writing Smart Junior

Business School Companion
College Companion
Law School Companion
Medical School Companion

Student Access Guide to College Admissions
Student Advantage Guide to the Best 310 Colleges
Student Advantage Guide to America's Top Internships
Student Advantage Guide to Business Schools
Student Advantage Guide to Law Schools
Student Advantage Guide to Medical Schools
Student Advantage Guide to Paying for College
Student Advantage Guide to Summer
Student Advantage Guide to Visiting College Campuses
Student Advantage Guide: Help Yourself
Student Advantage Guide: The Complete Book of Colleges
Student Advantage Guide: The Internship Bible
Hillel Guide to Jewish Life on Campus
International Students' Guide to the United States
The Princeton Review Guide to Your Career

Also available on cassette from Living Language
Grammar Smart
Word Smart
Word Smart II

THE PRINCETON REVIEW

Biology Smart

BY DEBORAH GUEST

Random House, Inc.
New York 1996
http://www.randomhouse.com

Princeton Review Publishing, L.L.C.
2315 Broadway, 3rd Floor
New York, NY 10024
E-mail: info@review.com

ISBN 0-679-76908-0

Edited by: Amy Zavatto
Designed by: Illeny Maaza
Illustrations by: John Bergdahl and The Production Department of The Princeton Review

Manufactured in the United States of America on recycled paper.

9 8 7 6 5 4 3 2 1

First Edition

ACKNOWLEDGMENTS

I would like to thank the staff at The Princeton Review for their assistance in writing *Biology Smart:* Amy Zavatto, Ken Howard, Bruno Blumenfeld, John Bergdahl, Illeny Mazza, John Pak, Effie Hadjiioannou, Julian Heath, Greta Englert, Matthew Reilly. I also want to include John Katzman, for offering me this book. Thanks.

DEDICATION

This book is dedicated to the memory of Dr. Peter Sajovic, who had the mind and passion of a true biologist, along with a wicked sense of humor. What's more, he believed in people.

CONTENTS

1

General Chemistry

THE PERIODIC TABLE OF THE ELEMENTS

Everyone knows what a diamond ring looks like.

If you were asked to describe what a diamond ring is made of, you'd probably say something like this:

> "Well, it's made of metal and a cut stone called a diamond."

Of course, your answer would be right. But if we told you that the metal is made of gold or maybe platinum (if it's extra fancy), and the stone is made of nothing but carbon, we'd be right, too. That's because all objects are made of building blocks called *elements*. The Periodic Table of the Elements lists all of the possible known elements that something can be made out of. You won't find "gold" listed there, though. Nor will you find the words "platinum" or "carbon." Instead you'll find the *symbol* for gold (Au), platinum (Pt), and carbon (C). Each element on the Periodic Table is known by the symbol that chemists assign to it.

1																	18
1 H 1.0																	2 He 4.0
3 Li 6.9	4 Be 9.0											5 B 10.8	6 C 12.0	7 N 14.0	8 O 16.0	9 F 19.0	10 Ne 20.2
11 Na 23.0	12 Mg 24.3											13 Al 27.0	14 Si 28.1	15 P 31.0	16 S 32.1	17 Cl 35.5	18 Ar 39.9
19 K 39.1	20 Ca 40.1	21 Sc 45.0	22 Ti 47.9	23 V 50.9	24 Cr 52.0	25 Mn 54.9	26 Fe 55.8	27 Co 58.9	28 Ni 58.7	29 Cu 63.5	30 Zn 65.4	31 Ga 69.7	32 Ge 72.6	33 As 74.9	34 Se 79.0	35 Br 79.9	36 Kr 83.8
37 Rb 85.5	38 Sr 87.6	39 Y 88.9	40 Zr 91.2	41 Nb 92.9	42 Mo 95.9	43 Te (98)	44 Ru 101.1	45 Rh 102.9	46 Pd 106.4	47 Ag 107.9	48 Cd 112.4	49 In 114.8	50 Sn 118.7	51 Sb 121.8	52 Te 127.6	53 I 126.9	54 Xe 131.3
55 Cs 132.9	56 Ba 137.3	57 La 138.9	72 Hf 178.5	73 Ta 180.9	74 W 183.9	75 Re 186.2	76 Os 190.2	77 Ir 192.2	78 Pt 195.1	79 Au 197.0	80 Hg 200.6	81 Tl 204.4	82 Pb 207.2	83 Bi 209.0	84 Po (209)	85 At (210)	86 Rn (222)
87 Fr (223)	88 Ra 226.0	89 Ac 227.0	104 Unq (261)	105 Unp (262)	106 Unh (263)	107 Uns (262)	108 Uno (265)	109 Une (267)									

58 Ce 140.1	59 Pr 140.9	60 Nd 144.2	61 Pm (145)	62 Sm 150.4	63 Eu 152.0	64 Gd 157.3	65 Tb 158.9	66 Dy 162.5	67 Ho 164.9	68 Er 167.3	69 Tm 168.9	70 Yb 173.0	71 Lu 175.0
90 Th 232.0	91 Pa (231)	92 U 238.0	93 Np (237)	94 Pu (244)	95 Am (243)	96 Cm (247)	97 Bk (247)	98 Cr (251)	99 Es (252)	100 Fm (257)	101 Md (258)	102 No (259)	103 Lr (260)

So, now you know that all things are made up of one or more of the elements listed in the Periodic Table of the Elements. When we say "things," we mean everything you could possibly think of—like inanimate objects you can touch (solids), living organisms like us, slippery substances like water (liquids), and even stuff you can't see, like air (gases).

Since this isn't a book about chemistry, we're happy to tell you that you don't need to learn all 109 elements of the Periodic Table.

You just have to know a few. For instance, let's look at these 4 elements:

1	2	3	4	5	6	7	8	9	10	11	12	13	14	15	16	17	18
1 H 1.008																	2
3	4											5	6 C 12.001	7 N 14.01	8 O 16.00	9	10
11	12											13	14	15	16	17	18
19	20	21	22	23	24	25	26	27	28	29	30	31	32	33	34	35	36
37	38	39	40	41	42	43	44	45	46	47	48	49	50	51	52	53	54
55	56	57	72	73	74	75	76	77	78	79	80	81	82	83	84	85	86
87	88	89	104	105	106	107	108	109									

58	59	60	61	62	63	64	65	66	67	68	69	70	71
90	91	92	93	94	95	96	97	98	99	100	101	102	103

- The H stands for hydrogen.
- The C stands for carbon.
- The O stands for oxygen.
- The N stands for nitrogen.

Why do you have to know these particular elements? Because they are extremely important in biology, which you'll see in a minute.

MADAM, I'M AN ATOM

Are elements as small as things can get? No—the smallest whole unit of an element is the *atom*. One atom of something has:

I. A nucleus.

Inside the nucleus are two things: 1. a *neutron* has a mass, but no charge to it—it's neutral—and, 2. a *proton* carries a positive charge.

So far then, it looks like an atom has an overall positive charge—because its nucleus contains an equal number of neutral charges (the neutron) and positive charges (+, the proton). But we're not done yet. An atom also contains something else:

II. Electrons.

Electrons are outside the nucleus, but they are still a part of the atom. They have a lot of mobility out there, and they make use of it. Each electron carries a negative charge (–). Normally, there are as many electrons in an atom as there are protons and neutrons. This makes the average atom neutral in charge.

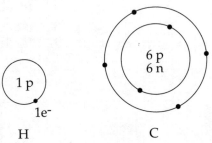

ABOUT HYDROGEN

Hydrogen does not have a neutron in its nucleus. It has one proton there and it has one electron outside of its nucleus.

Another thing about hydrogen: it's involved in pH measurements. The concentration of H^+s that are around help to determine what the *pH* of something is. (H^+ stands for hydrogen *ion*. An ion is the name for an atom that carries a charge. The charge can be either positive or negative.) The measure of pH kind of weighs how many H^+s are around against how many OH^-s are around. The *pH scale* ranges from 1 to 14.

A pH of 1 is seriously *acidic* (meaning there are lots of H^+s around).

A pH of 7 is *neutral* (meaning there are equal amounts of H^+s and OH^-s around).

A pH of 14 is seriously alkaline or basic (meaning there are lots of OH^-s around).

Consider This

Blood, for instance, is on the alkaline side, so you know right away that its pH is more than 7.0 and there are more OH^-s in it than there are H^+s. Urine, on the other hand, is on the acidic side, so you know that its pH is below 7.0 and there are more H^+s in it than there are OH^-s.

So an atom has neutrons and protons in its nucleus and electrons outside its nucleus. Why should you know this stuff? Because when we look at these small pieces of an atom, we get an idea of how *bonds* form between atoms. And you need to understand some things about bonds in order to understand biology.

LET'S TALK ABOUT BONDS

Bonds are drawn like this: (—). Water, for instance, can be written as H_2O. This shows its *molecular formula*: water is composed of two hydrogen molecules and one oxygen molecule. Water can also be written as

$$H \diagdown \quad H \diagup$$
$$O$$

This shows water's *structural* arrangement, or how the atoms actually bond with one another to form a water molecule. From this we can see that, in a water molecule, hydrogen atoms bond to an oxygen atom and not to each other. Each single bond in the picture indicates that two electrons are being shared between the atoms that form the bonds.

FYI

The most number of bonds that can be formed around one carbon (C), nitrogen (N), or oxygen (O) atom is four:

$$-\overset{|}{\underset{|}{C}}- \qquad -\overset{|}{N}- \qquad -\overset{|}{\underset{|}{O}}-$$

The most number of bonds that can be formed around one hydrogen atom is one:

$$H-$$

Single bonds are not the only type of sharing that atoms can practice. A double bond can also be formed, as you will see in the case of amino acids in chapter two. In a *double* bond, four electrons are shared. *Triple* bonds are also allowed (here 6 electrons are shared by two atoms). Double and triple bonds are okay in atomic bonding as long as there's a maximum of only four bonds for any given atom (besides hydrogen, of course, since we said that it can form only one bond), giving a total of eight shared electrons.

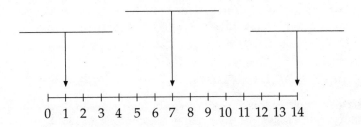

pH Scale

1. Label the arrows shown on the pH scale above using the following terms:

    I. highly acidic
    II. highly alkaline
    III. neutral

2. True or False: A weak base contains more H^+ ions than it does OH^- ions.

    _____

3. Which is a stronger acid, hydrochloric acid at pH 1.0, or vinegar at pH 3.0?

    _____

4. Citric acid is found in citrus fruits such as oranges and grapefruits. What approximate value do you think it would have on a pH scale?

    A. Between 0 and 7
    B. Precisely 7.0
    C. Between 7 and 14
    D. Precisely 14.0

Questions 5 through 9 refer to the molecule shown below.

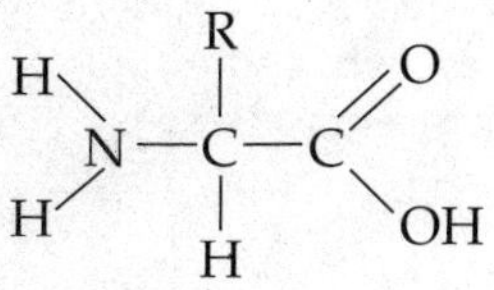

5. How many bonds are formed around nitrogen (N)?

_____

6. How many double bonds are present in the entire molecule?

_____

7. How many bonds are formed around any one hydrogen (H) atom?

_____

8. How many bonds surround each carbon (C) atom?

_____

9. The section COOH refers to which portion of the structure?

   A. The left
   B. The right
   C. The middle
   D. None of the above

Meet the Bonds

You've probably heard of James Bond. We want to introduce you to some other members of the Bond family.
The **covalent** bond—when two atoms share electrons equally.
The **ionic** bond—when one atom transfers an electron to another atom.
The **hydrogen** bond—when a hydrogen atom is shared between two atoms.

HYDROGEN BONDS

A hydrogen bond is considered a weak bond. Let's take a look why. The two water molecules below are each composed of two hydrogen atoms co-valently bonded to an oxygen atom.

If we bring these two water molecules closer to each other, something interesting starts to happen. The hydrogen atom in molecule 1 becomes attracted to the oxygen atom in molecule 2. Don't forget that a hydrogen atom can only form one covalent bond with another atom—and it's already attached to an oxygen atom within its own molecule. But that doesn't stop it from gravitating towards its neighboring oxygen. How does it resolve its dilemma? It forms a hydrogen bond with the neighboring oxygen. By con-vention, the hydrogen bond is depicted as a broken line while the covalent bond is shown as a solid line.

So there you have it—an example of a hydrogen bond as we have defined it above. In this case, the hydrogen atom is shared between the oxygen of water molecule 1 and the oxygen of water molecule 2.

Interesting Facts about Hydrogen Bonds

1. They often form at oxygen or nitrogen atoms.
2. They're super-important in biological systems.
3. They form and break up rather easily.
4. They may be weak singly, but cumulatively they are s-t-r-o-n-g.

Hydrogen Bonds and Surface Tension

Imagine yourself preparing to execute the perfect dive. Imagine yourself poised at the edge of the diving board, muscles taut, feet flexed to become airborne. Imagine your launch from the board in one fluid motion. Now imagine your flawless swan dive turning midair into a belly flop, and imagine the slap of pain you feel as you enter the water. Countless hydrogen bonds that form between individual water molecules produce *surface tension*. The surface tension is strong enough to allow water insects to ride the water's surface like a freeway and to greet your dive with a wall of resistance.

Check Your Progress 2
Questions 1 and 2 refer to the picture shown below.

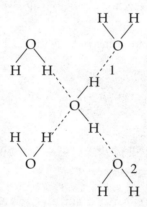

I. Covalent bond
II. Ionic bond
III. Hydrogen bond

Identify the correct type of bond indicated by filling in the blank with the appropriate answer.

1. Bond 1 _____

2. Bond 2 _____

3. The surface tension of water is produced by the interaction of numerous

    A. covalent bonds
    B. ionic bonds
    C. hydrogen bonds
    D. peptide bonds

GLOSSARY

acidic
:   something that releases hydrogen ions; registers below 7 on a pH scale

alkaline
:   (a.k.a. base) something that releases OH ions; registers above 7 on a pH scale

atom
:   the smallest whole part of an element; contains protons, neutrons, and electrons

bond
:   a force that keeps two nearby atoms connected to each other

covalent bond
:   the equal sharing of electrons between atoms

electron
:   a subparticle of an atom; it lies outside the nucleus and carries a negative charge

element
:   the most basic ingredient of something; it cannot be separated into anything other than itself

hydrogen bond
:   a weak bond; it happens when hydrogen is shared between two atoms (usually O or N)

ion
:   an atom that carries either a positive (+) or negative (–) charge

ionic bond
:   electrons are not equally shared in this type of bond: an electron is closer to one atom than to the other in the association

neutron
:   a subparticle of an atom; it lies in the nucleus and has a mass but carries no charge

pH
:   a measure of how acidic or basic something is

pH scale
:   ranges from 0 (strongly acidic, strong H^+ ion concentration) to 14 (strongly basic, strong OH^- ion concentration); a pH of 7 is neutral

proton
:   a subparticle of an atom; it lies within the nucleus and carries a positive charge

surface tension
:   hydrogen bonding helps water molecules stick tightly to one another, creating a tension at the water's surface

ANSWER KEY

Check Your Progress 1

1. I, III, II
2. false
3. hydrochloric acid
4. A
5. 3
6. 1
7. 1
8. 4
9. B

Check Your Progress 2

1. III
2. I
3. C

2

Organic Chemistry I

SUGARS, CARBOHYDRATES, LIPIDS, AND PROTEINS

Now that you've got the basics of chemistry down, we're ready to get into some organic chemistry.

WHAT DOES "ORGANIC" MEAN?

The term "organic" means different things to different people. To a farmer, "organic" means a method of farming that minimizes the use of synthetic fertilizers, pesticides, and herbicides. To an artist who describes the "organic" process that went into creating a piece of artwork, who knows what he means by "organic." Your guess is as good as ours.

To biologists, however (and that means you), "organic" has a precise meaning that never varies. When we talk about organic molecules in biology, we apply a simple, down-to-earth criterion of just what we mean by "organic":

The flip side of this assessment, of course, is: if it doesn't contain carbon, then it's not organic. The word for "not organic" is *inorganic*.

There's No Such Thing as a Free Lunch

Let's recap: Say you're standing in line at the cafeteria and in your hapless position your science teacher spots you, heads over, presents you with a picture of a horrific-looking structure of some molecule you've never seen before, and demands to know whether or not it's organic before you can order your lunch. You don't even sweat it, because you know what to do.

You ask yourself, "Does it contain carbon?" You then look for one or more Cs (the symbol that stands for carbon) in the picture. If you spot any Cs, you definitely answer that the molecule is organic. If you don't spot any Cs, you conclude that it's inorganic. You've made your teacher very happy and now you can get back to your lunch.

CHECK YOUR PROGRESS 1

For questions 1-4, identify each of the following molecular structures as either "organic" or "inorganic."

1.
$$\begin{array}{c} H \\ | \\ H-C-H \\ | \\ H \end{array}$$
_____

2. H—Cl
_____

3.
$$\begin{array}{c} H \quad H \\ \diagdown \diagup \\ O \end{array}$$
_____

4.

H
|
H—C—OH
C————O
H   H
C   C
HO   C———C   OH
| |
H   OH

SACCHARIDES

Let's consider for a moment one organic molecule that most people know and love. People spoon it into their coffee, drink it out of soda cans, and even get it intravenously at hospitals. It tastes good, it rots the teeth, it replenishes energy, it's fattening, it inspires imitations, and it's everywhere. It's sugar. Another name for it is *glucose*, whose molecular formula is $C_6H_{12}O_6$. *Fructose* is also a sugar, as is *sucrose* and *maltose*, to name a few more. Six-carbon sugars are called *hexoses*. Five-carbon sugars are called *pentoses*. Notice anything that sugars have in common?

1. Compounds ending in "ose" are sugars—and there are quite a few sugars out there.

2. Sugars are made up of the elements C, H, and O.

3. In sugars, the ratio of H to O is usually 2:1.

What else can we say about sugars? Well, they're also called *saccharides*. There are *monosaccharides* (like glucose), which are made up of one sugar molecule, and there are *disaccharides* (like maltose), which are made up of two sugar molecules.

Here are a few examples of monosaccharides:

• glucose
• fructose

and some examples of disaccharides:

• lactose
• sucrose
• maltose

DEHYDRATION SYNTHESIS

If you want to create a disaccharide from two monosaccharides, you remove one molecule of water. This process is called (logically enough) *dehydration synthesis*. The dehydration part is the removal of water. The synthesis part is the joining of the two smaller compounds to create one larger one.

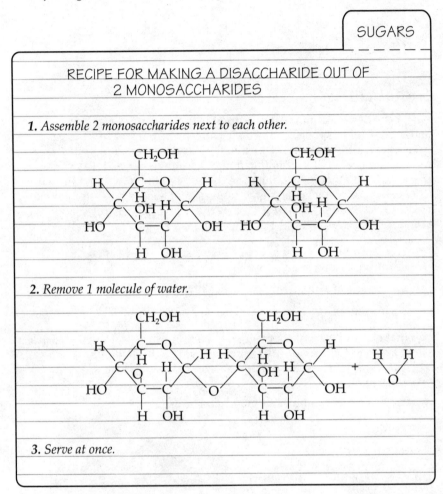

RECIPE FOR MAKING A DISACCHARIDE OUT OF 2 MONOSACCHARIDES

1. Assemble 2 monosaccharides next to each other.

2. Remove 1 molecule of water.

3. Serve at once.

WHEN YOU CAN'T STOP

So if you want to join up two monosaccharides, you just remove a molecule of water. Let's say you don't want to stop there. Can you keep on adding monosaccharides one by one via dehydration synthesis? Sure—only you won't have a disaccharide anymore as your product. Instead you'll get a *polysaccharide*. Lots of glucose molecules strung together makes a polysaccharide.

Below are some examples of polysaccharides:

- starches (source of energy)
- glycogen (concentrated form of sugar)
- cellulose (found in plant cell walls)

HYDROLYSIS

Now let's think about reversing the synthesis process. What if you have a disaccharide, but what you really want are two monosaccharides? Can you break the disaccharide into smaller units? Yes, you can—but not by using dehydration synthesis, of course. Instead you perform in effect the reverse of dehydration synthesis. You *add* a molecule of water to break down the disaccharide. Any time that you add a molecule of water to break a bond, you're performing *hydrolysis*.

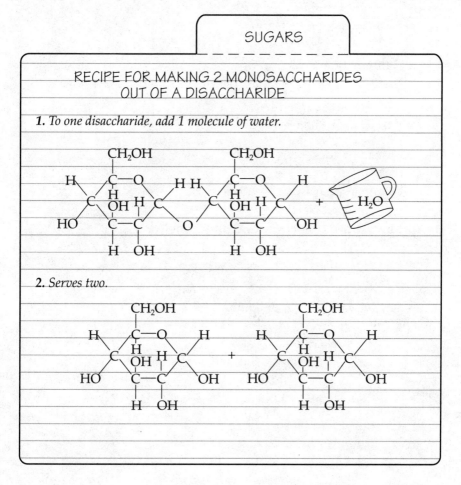

SUGARS

RECIPE FOR MAKING 2 MONOSACCHARIDES OUT OF A DISACCHARIDE

1. *To one disaccharide, add 1 molecule of water.*

2. *Serves two.*

WHAT'S A CARBOHYDRATE?

A *carbohydrate* is made up only of carbons (Cs), oxygens (Os), and hydrogens (Hs). But wait—didn't we say that that's what sugar molecules were made of? We did—it turns out that sugar molecules are carbohydrates. So are starches, or polysaccharides. With all of these new terms to get down, we'd better review.

Body Fuel

"Saccharide" is another word for "sugar."
A monosaccharide is one simple sugar molecule.
A disaccharide is made up of two sugar molecules.
A polysaccharide is a whole string of sugar molecules.
"Starch" is type of "polysaccharide."
A carbohydrate is a sugar or a starch, and it's made up of Cs, Hs, and Os.

CHECK YOUR PROGRESS 2

For questions 1-4, fill in the following blanks with either answer choice I or II.

> I. Hydrolysis
> II. Dehydration synthesis

1. Disaccharide → 2 monosaccharides   _____

2. 2 monosaccharides → disaccharide   _____

3. Involves the removal of a water molecule   _____

4. Involves the addition of a water molecule   _____

So now we know about an entire class of organic compounds called carbohydrates (sugars and starches). What's next?

LIPIDS

You may have heard of a medical procedure called "liposuction," in which a doctor can suction off extra fat from areas of the body that tend to store fat. So why isn't the technique called "fatosuction?" Because fats belong to a class of compounds called *lipids*. Following are a few examples of lipids:

- fats

- oils

- waxes

- cholesterol

Like carbohydrates, lipids are made up of carbons, hydrogens, and oxygens. Unlike carbohydrate's ratio of 2:1, however, the ratio in a lipid is a whole lot more than 2 hydrogens for each oxygen present.

For instance, a glucose molecule has 12 hydrogens and 6 oxygens (that's a 2:1 ratio). Now look at this picture of a lipid molecule:

This intimidating-looking lipid molecule (called a *triglyceride*) has more than 36 hydrogens and only 6 oxygens! (That's our greater than 2:1 ratio). A triglyceride is made up of 3 *fatty acids* and 1 *glycerol* molecule. We're sorry, but you have to know that. The broken lines shown in the fatty acids is shorthand for saying that many more *hydrocarbons* (Cs with Hs attached) belong in the picture. You also should recognize which section is the glycerol and which sections are the fatty acids when you eyeball one of these lipids.

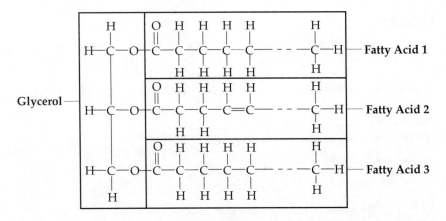

So what's so great about lipids? Well, for starters they are a form of stored energy for living things. They are also an essential part of each one of our cell membranes.

CHECK YOUR PROGRESS 3

1. Which one of the following correctly lists the ratio of hydrogens to oxygens in a lipid?

   A. 1:2
   B. >1:2
   C. 2:1
   D. >2:1

2. The elements carbon, hydrogen, and oxygen are the sole building blocks of

   A. sugars only
   B. lipids only
   C. carbohydrates only
   D. carbohydrates and lipids

3. All of the following are lipids EXCEPT

   A. fats
   B. cholesterol
   C. sugars
   D. waxes

4. All of the following are carbohydrates EXCEPT

   A. glycogen
   B. cellulose
   C. starches
   D. oils

5. A compound containing three fatty acids and a glycerol is called

   A. a triglyceride
   B. a wax
   C. glycogen
   D. cellulose

WHAT'S AN AMINO ACID?

Another class of molecules you need to know about are *amino acids*. The generic amino acid looks like this:

Unlike the triglyceride, which you need to recognize only superficially, the amino acid is one compound that you'll need to know more intimately. For starters, you should be able to recognize the parts of an amino acid. Most notable are:

1. the *amino group*, NH_2

2. the *carboxyl group*, COOH

3. the *R group*, varies—can be any one of 20 different pieces

The R group stands for the amino acid's *sidechain*. The structure of the sidechain is different for each different amino acid. There are 20 different amino acids, and there are 20 different sidechains that make those amino acids different from one another.

FYI

Did you know that the simplest sidechain is H, and it belongs to the amino acid *glycine*? A more complex sidechain is $H_2NCH_2CH_2CH_2CH_2$, and it belongs to *lysine*.

HERE WE GO AGAIN

Amino acids are the building blocks of proteins. Two amino acids joined together are called a *dipeptide*, and three or more amino acids strung together are called a *polypeptide*. To form a dipeptide from two amino acids, we take away one molecule of water. If you're thinking right now, "Hey, isn't that dehydration synthesis?" you're right. Let's take a closer look at how a dipeptide is made:

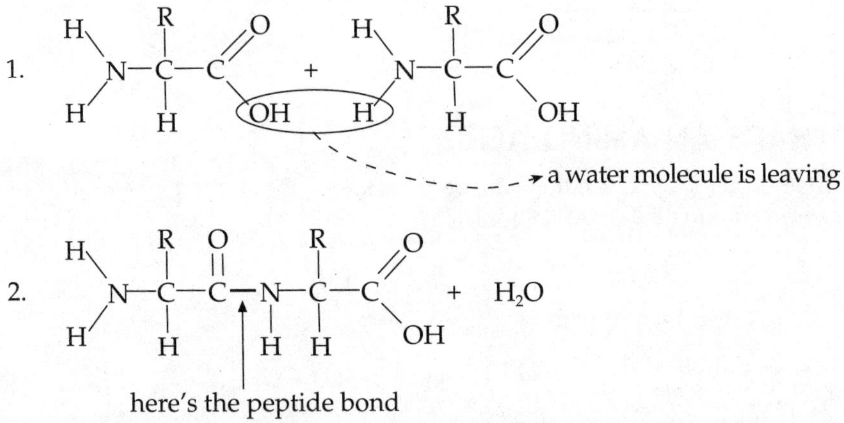

1.
$$H_2N-\underset{\underset{H}{|}}{\overset{\overset{R}{|}}{C}}-C\overset{O}{\underset{OH}{\diagup}} \quad + \quad H_2N-\underset{\underset{H}{|}}{\overset{\overset{R}{|}}{C}}-C\overset{O}{\underset{OH}{\diagup}}$$

- - - → a water molecule is leaving

2.
$$H_2N-\underset{\underset{H}{|}}{\overset{\overset{R}{|}}{C}}-\overset{\overset{O}{||}}{C}-N-\underset{\underset{H}{|}}{\overset{\overset{R}{|}}{C}}-C\overset{O}{\underset{OH}{\diagup}} \quad + \quad H_2O$$

here's the peptide bond

On the other hand, the process of hydrolysis will dispatch with amino acids one by one off of a dipeptide or polypeptide.

THE PEPTIDE BOND

The bond that forms the dipeptide is called a *peptide bond*. Where is it? Between the carboxyl group (COOH) of the first amino acid and the amino group (NH$_2$) of the second amino acid.

CHECK YOUR PROGRESS 4

1. Draw a box around the peptide bond in the dipeptide pictured below.

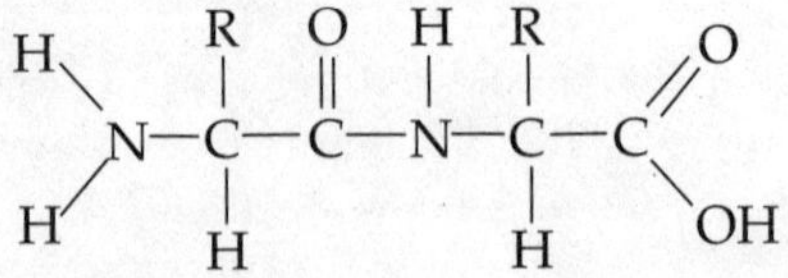

$$H_2N-\underset{\underset{H}{|}}{\overset{\overset{R}{|}}{C}}-\overset{\overset{O}{||}}{C}-\underset{\underset{H}{|}}{\overset{\overset{H}{|}}{N}}-\underset{\underset{H}{|}}{\overset{\overset{R}{|}}{C}}-C\overset{O}{\underset{OH}{\diagup}}$$

2. Which of the following correctly depicts a peptide bond?
   A. CR—CO
   B. NH$_2$—CR
   C. CO—NH
   D. NH—CR

3. A dipeptide is created via

   A. hydrolysis
   B. dehydration synthesis
   C. hydrogen bonding
   D. none of the above

4. A protein is unique from lipids and carbohydrates in that it contains

   A. carbon
   B. oxygen
   C. nitrogen
   D. hydrogen

5. Draw in the amino group in the circles drawn in the picture shown below of an amino acid.

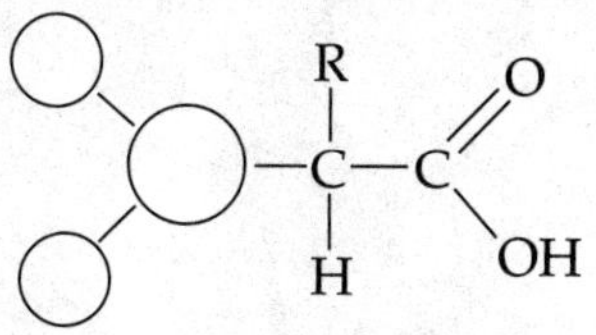

6. Draw in the carboxyl group in circles drawn in the picture shown below of an amino acid.

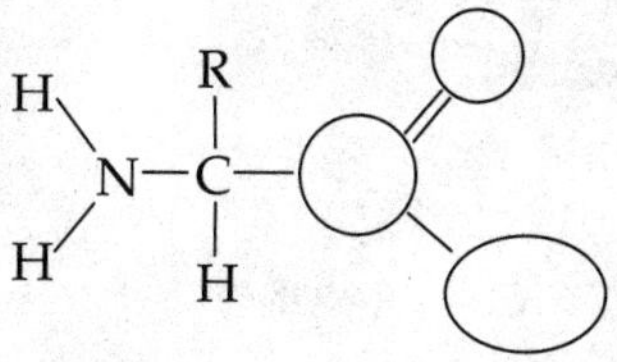

Some polypeptides are proteins. The string of polypeptides folds up in special ways that are determined by interactions of its atoms. By folding up in specific formations, the protein takes on its three-dimensional shape, and also its function. Take a look at the protein presented below. It's folded up in neat ways thanks to bonds formed between the amino acids *cysteine* (cys) found throughout the polypeptide.

Lys – Glu – Thr – Ala – Ala – Ala – Lys – Phe – Glu – Arg – Glu – His – Met
5 ... 10
Asp
Ser 15
Met – Met – Glu – Asn – Cys – Tyr – Asn – Ser – Ser – Ser – Ala – Ala – Ser – Thr – Ser
30 ... 25 ... 20
Lys
Thr – Glu – Arg – Cys – Asp – Thr – Ile – Ser – Met – Thr – Ser – Tyr – Ser – Glu – Tyr
85 ... 80 ... 75
Ser Gly
Arg Ser   Asn – Cys
Asn Ser   70 Thr   Cys 65
35 Leu Ser 90   Glu   Ala
Thr Lys 124   120   Gly – Asn – Lys Val
Lys Tyr Val – Ser – Ala – Asp – Phe – His – Val – Pro – Val – Tyr – Pro – Asn – Gly Asn
Asp Pro   115   Glu Lys
Arg Asn   110 Cys Glu 60
40 Cys 95   Ala Ser
Cys – Ala – Tyr – Lys – Thr – Thr – Glu – Ala – Asn – Lys – His – Ile – Ile Val
100 ... 105
Cys – Lys – Pro – Val – Asn – Thr – Phe – Val – His – Glu – Ser – Leu – Ala – Asp – Val – Glu – Ala – Val – Cys
45 ... 50 ... 55

The protein's name is *bovine pancreatic ribonuclease A*. Do you have to remember that? No. You don't have to memorize a thing about this protein. Instead you can just appreciate its looks.

PROTEINS—1001 USES AND COUNTING

Amino acids are a big deal in biology because they constitute the building blocks of proteins. An advertiser would have a field day extolling the many virtues of the protein. There are many different proteins in an organism and they carry out all sorts of different jobs.

The protein *hemoglobin* functions to transport oxygen in red blood cells. *Antibodies* are another class of proteins that help the body to fight off infections. *Keratin*, a protein found in hair and nails, provides structural support. The protein *insulin* acts as a hormone in the body. Integral and peripheral proteins found in and around the cell membrane act as gatekeepers, regulating what leaves and enters the cell.

These glimpses into the multifaceted protein are not your last, by the way, so don't worry about memorizing them here. You'll meet proteins pretty frequently as we cover more of biology. It just goes to show how essential proteins are in the lives of organisms.

GLOSSARY

amino acid
the basic building block of a protein, contains an amino group and a carboxyl group

amino group
made up of NH_2; found in amino acids

carbohydrate
includes sugars and starches; made up only of C, H and O; the H to O ratio is 2:1

carboxyl group
made up of COOH; found in amino acids

cellulose
a carbohydrate; found in plant cell walls

dehydration synthesis
the formation of a larger molecule from two smaller ones via removal of a molecule of water

dipeptide
consists of two amino acids joined by a peptide bond

disaccharide
consists of two simple sugar molecules joined together

glycogen
a carbohydrate made up of many glucose molecules; used to store energy

hydrolysis
the breaking of a larger molecule into two smaller ones by adding a molecule of water

inorganic
any molecule that does not contain carbon

lipid
a class of organic compounds that includes fats, oils, and waxes; H to O ratio is >2:1

monosaccharide
any sugar molecule with the formula $C_nH_{2n}O_n$

organic
any molecule that contains carbon

peptide bond
the bond joining the carboxyl group of one amino acid with the amino group of the next amino acid

polypeptide
consists of many amino acids joined together by peptide bonds; proteins are polypeptides

polysaccharide
consists of many simple sugar molecules joined together; includes glycogen, starches, and cellulose

protein
a compound made up of one or more polypeptides

R group
the variable group on an amino acid; stands for any one of 20 different structures

saccharide
a sugar

sidechain
the variable group that makes up the R group on an amino acid; there are 20 to choose from

starch
a carbohydrate

triglyceride
a type of lipid made up of one glycerol and three fatty acids

ANSWER KEY

Check Your Progress 1

1. organic

2. inorganic

3. inorganic

4. organic

Check Your Progress 2

1. I

2. II

3. II

4. I

Check Your Progress 3

1. D

2. D

3. C

4. D

5. A

Check Your Progress 4

1.

2. C

3. B

4. C

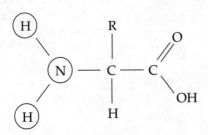

6.

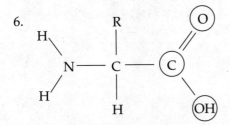

CHAPTER 3

Organic Chemistry II

ENZYMES

One class of proteins is so important that it gets an entire section devoted to it. We're talking about *enzymes* here. What makes them so hot? It's because of what they do. They make reactions in a cell happen a whole lot faster than they otherwise would have. It's like this: molecules A and B are just sitting around in the cell and they *could* undergo a reaction to produce C.

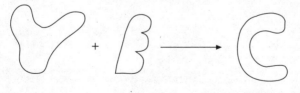

    molecule A   molecule B   product C

Just because reactants A and B could undergo a reaction, however, doesn't mean that they will anytime soon. Here lies the crux of an enzyme's job: an enzyme speeds up the rate of a reaction.

Does an enzyme make a reaction happen that otherwise would never, ever have happened? No. Does it make the reaction churn out more products? Nope. Does it alter the steps of the reaction itself in any way? No. So what does an enzyme do again? An enzyme simply allows a reaction that *could* have happened anyway to happen *faster*.

It's kind of like this: say you know that your friend in Kansas would really like your friend in Georgia and vice versa. Chances are, if left to fate, these two friends of yours would never meet up with one another, even though if they did, they'd really hit it off. So you intervene by getting them together. You invite them both over to your house. They both come to see you, and in the process they meet each other. It didn't cost you anything to get them together, and sure enough, when they meet each other they form this awesome friendship.

WHY ENZYMES ARE CRITICALLY IMPORTANT TO A CELL

A cell can't afford to sit around forever waiting for a reaction to happen on its own sweet time. Instead the cell produces enzymes that get the reactants to react. This way the cell can carry on with all of its reactions, which keep it alive.

Let's look more closely at one hypothetical reaction that creates product C, which the cell simply must have in order to thrive.

$$\text{Reactants A + B} \rightarrow \text{Product C}$$

Say that the cell needs some product C and it needs it now. What does it do? It manufactures some enzyme Z. Why? So that Z can get reactants A and B together to produce C. Mission accomplished.

$$\text{Reactants A + B + Enzyme Z} \rightarrow \text{Product C + Enzyme Z}$$

Now let's say that the cell has plenty of C and really can't handle any more of it for a while. What does it do? It can cut down on production of enzyme Z. Without so much enzyme Z around to facilitate matters, the reaction rate slows down and less Cs get made.

So enzymes are actually an ingenious tool used by the cell to fine tune its activities and production lines.

Here's something else to think about that is nice and straightforward. Sometimes enzymes are helped in performing their job. Their assistants are called *coenzymes*. Vitamins act as coenzymes.

1. An enzymatic reaction that is provided with sufficient enzymes and substrates most likely occurs

    A. once in a blue moon
    B. never
    C. rarely
    D. readily

2. Enzymes speed up the _____ of a reaction.

3. Which of the following act as coenzymes?

    A. lipids
    B. peptides
    C. vitamins
    D. minerals

HOW DOES AN ENZYME WORK?

Since an enzyme is a protein, we know that it's made up of amino acids joined together by peptide bonds and that the polypeptide is then folded up into some three-dimensional shape.

Now here's what's special about an enzyme's shape: it has what is called an *active site*. The active site is like a dock where *reactants* (also called *substrates*) can temporarily anchor themselves. There's a special binding site for two or more substrates on the enzyme's active site. Now let's think about this for a minute. If, say, there are two boats out on the sea somewhere, it's pretty unlikely that by chance they will even get within sight of one another. After all, the sea's a pretty big place and two boats are comparatively small.

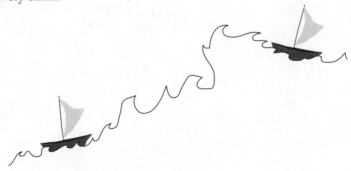

But if both boats happen to pull up at the same dock to moor, well, now they're positioned right next to one another, in adjacent boat slips.

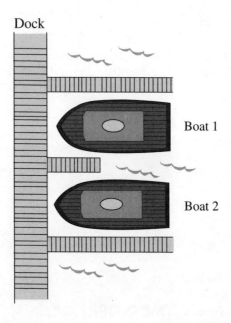

Dock

Boat 1

Boat 2

Enzymes act as the dock, and the binding sites on their active sites act as the boat slips. The substrates act as the boats and the entire intracellular space can be thought of as the sea. The substrates would have a hard time finding one another in the open sea that is the intracellular space. So an enzyme acts as a temporary docking site, bringing the substrates in close to one another. The close proximity of the substrates initiates the reaction.

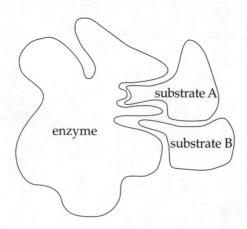

enzyme

substrate A

substrate B

What happens to all of the players once the reaction is over?

1. The reactants don't exist anymore. (Substrates A and B are now history.)

2. Product C appears.

3. The enzyme is left exactly the same as it was before the reaction took place.

PORTRAIT OF AN ENZYME

Think of the enzyme as the Dorian Gray of the biochemical world (without the specter of a hideous portrait to haunt it), unmarred by life, entering into reactions over and over without seeming to suffer any consequences.

This ability of an enzyme to speed up the rate of a reaction without itself being changed has earned it the name of *organic catalyst*. You already know what organic means (it contains carbon). A catalyst is something that effects a change in something, but is not itself changed in the process.

CHECK YOUR PROGRESS 2

Answer "yes" or "no" to the following set of questions.

1. Can an enzyme be used more than once in a reaction? _____

2. Does an enzyme undergo change during a reaction? _____

3. Is an enzyme an organic catalyst? _____

4. Does an enzyme slow the rate of a reaction? _____

5. Are reactants A and B present after a reaction has occurred? _____

6. Is a substrate also a reactant? _____

7. Does an enzyme allow the cell a measure of control over which reactions will take place when? _____

8. Does an enzyme work by bringing the products of a reaction close to one another? _____

ENZYME SPECIFICITY

If you can realize that a square and a moon shape can't fit together, then you understand the concept of *enzyme specificity*. The shape of the enzyme allows it its function by determining what substrate will bind to it. For instance, a triangular-shaped substrate won't fit into a round active site. A square substrate won't fit into a crescent-shaped active site.

Let's say that you have a normal-shaped car that looks something like this:

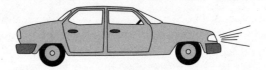

and your garage has a space that's shaped like this:

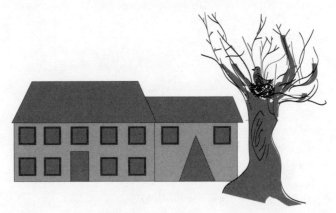

(Your architect was going through her "triangular phase" at the time.)

A lot of good your triangular garage does for you: your car can't fit into that space, so it stays outside under all those bird nests, getting wet, rusty, and covered with you-know-what. The car isn't the proper fit for the garage site, so the garage can't really work for that car.

If, during her triangular phase, the architect had also designed a *car* for you, there would be a happier ending to this story. This particular car would fit the garage site and the garage could do its job for that car.

THE LOCK-AND-KEY THEORY OF ENZYMES

Enzymes operate in the same way that our garage does. If a specific substrate does not fit the active site, then the substrate won't bind there and the enzyme won't catalyze that particular reaction. This concept is called the *lock-and-key theory*, which makes sense if you think about it. Only one key will fit a given lock. All those dips and grooves have to fit precisely in order to engage and allow the door to open. The grooves and dips in the enzyme's active site must match those in the substrate, or nothing happens.

If the substrate does precisely match the active site in shape, then we get what is called the *enzyme-substrate complex*. What is it? It's a single structure created by the temporary association of substrate with enzyme. As soon as the reactants do their thing, however, the enzyme-substrate complex disbands and we're left with enzyme and product—two separate structures.

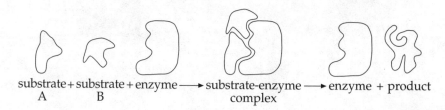

substrate + substrate + enzyme ⟶ substrate-enzyme ⟶ enzyme + product
    A   B   complex

CHECK YOUR PROGRESS 3

Fill in the blank in questions 1-4 by listing T for true and F for false.

1. A single enzyme is capable of catalyzing many different types of reactions. _____

2. A single enzyme is capable of catalyzing a specific reaction many times. _____

3. The enzyme-substrate complex is a transient structure that precedes formation of product in an enzymatic reaction. _____

4. The lock-and-key theory of enzymes attempts to explain an enzyme's specificity for a substrate. _____

AN ENZYME'S ACHILLES HEEL

So enzymes seem to be pretty amazing in the way in which they can catalyze a reaction over and over again without seeming to suffer any consequences. This might lead you to wonder if enzymes are indestructible. The answer is no. Eventually enzymes wear out. What's more, certain conditions actually stop an enzyme in its tracks:

1. high temperature
2. pH that is too high or too low

Here's where you ought to think of an enzyme not as an abstract thought, but as a real three-dimensional structure. Imagine that you are holding an enzyme between your palms (it's light-weight but awkwardly shaped) or walking around one and admiring it from all angles, as if it were a piece of artwork sitting on a table.

Enzyme A

KEEPING IN SHAPE IS SERIOUS BUSINESS TO AN ENZYME

An enzyme's ability to function depends in a big way on its three-dimensional shape. The bonds that form between atoms give the enzyme its shape. (Keep in mind here that the most important part of the enzyme is the active site, where the substrates actually bind.) It turns out that extremes in pH or temperature disrupts bonds. This alters the enzyme's *shape*, and therefore the enzyme's ability to *function*. After all, if the active site no longer has the right shape for its substrates to fit into, then the substrates can't bind. If the substrates can't bind, then they won't be brought close to one another, and the reaction won't happen.

FYI

Low temperature—makes the enzyme sluggish: it works, but more slowly than usual.

High temperature—is more disruptive; the heat actually breaks bonds (this process is called *denaturation*). When the bonds break, there goes the active site, and the enzyme is out of business, usually permanently.

Low or high pH—disrupts bonds, ruining the active site hence the enzyme's ability to function.

SATURATION KINETICS

Now that you've considered an enzyme in terms of its shape, let's think of it in its capacity as a worker. We said that each time it catalyzes one reaction, it:

1. binds to substrate A and substrate B
2. forms an enzyme-substrate complex
3. disbands, leaving the product and the enzyme in its original state.

So if we think about it, each time an enzyme is engaged with its substrate, it is unavailable to bind with more substrate. As soon as it disengages, of course, it is available and ready to catalyze another reaction by binding to more substrate. What we're talking about here is supply and demand.

WHEN THERE'S MORE ENZYME THAN SUBSTRATE

If you have 50 enzyme molecules and 20 substrate molecules for a given reaction, then even when all of the substrates are engaged, there are lots of enzymes that are not working. If the cell then produces more substrate molecules—say, 30 more—then all of the enzymes are now busy working, all of the substrates are engaged, and the number of times the reaction takes place goes up.

What happens if the cell adds even more substrate at this point?

WHEN THERE'S MORE SUBSTRATE THAN ENZYME

Now we have *over* 50 substrate molecules but only 50 enzymes. The enzyme is in demand (it's wanted by the other substrates) but it is already busy with its current substrate. The enzyme is now *saturated*.

About Saturation

When the sheer number of enzymes available to catalyze a reaction falls below the number of substrates that are waiting to bind, the enzymes are saturated.

No matter how many extra substrates get added at this point, the enzyme reaction rate remains the same, because the enzymes are already operating at maximum capacity.

With saturation, there are more substrates around than there are enzymes to deal with them. That means that the substrates basically have to wait their turn to be engaged with the next available enzyme. We all know what waiting for our turn is like. (And you probably never thought you could empathize with a substrate molecule.)

HERE'S OUR CHANCE TO PRACTICE READING A GRAPH

One skill you'll want to develop as you study biology is how to read graphs and charts. They come up pretty frequently in biology, and they're also handy in real life. It helps to know what you're looking at when you encounter one.

In this case we're going to look at a graph of how substrate concentration affects enzyme activity for a particular reaction. Here's the layout: on the horizontal axis (*x*-axis) we track the amount of substrate present; it increases as we move to the right. On the vertical axis (*y*-axis) we track enzymatic activity; it increases as we move up.

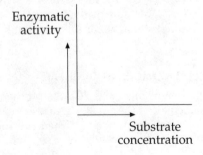

Now that we have a better handle on what it is we're measuring (enzymatic activity) against what (substrate concentration), we can take a look at the information that the graph provides.

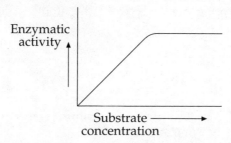

According to this graph, as substrate molecules are added, enzymatic activity goes up. (See for yourself—pick a spot about one-half an inch along the *x*-axis and then run your eye directly upwards from that spot. Take a look at where that lands you on the *y*-axis and mark it. Now do the same thing at the 1-inch mark. Notice that as you move upwards along the *x*-axis you also moved upwards along the *y*-axis? That means that as substrate increased, so did enzymatic activity.)

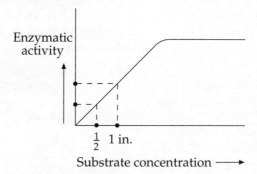

What happens, though, when you do the same thing further along the *x*-axis? When you match up two different points further on, signifying more substrate, you'll find that the enzymatic activity stays the same.

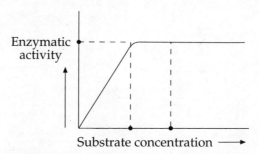

You've just identified the *saturation point* of this enzyme. At this point, additional substrate does not cause an increase in enzymatic activity.

Check Your Progress 4

1. List two conditions that destroy enzymatic activity by disrupting bonds between the atoms in an enzyme.

    1. _____

    2. _____

2. How do low and high temperature, respectively, affect an enzyme's function?

    low temperature:

    _____

    high temperature:

    _____

3. Say you are performing a laboratory experiment in your basement and you notice that if you add more substrate to your enzymatic reaction, you get more enzymatic activity. What can you conclude about the reaction?

    A. There is probably more substrate present than there is enzyme.
    B. There is probably more enzyme available than there is substrate.
    C. There is probably more product present than there is either substrate or enzyme.
    D. The enzyme-substrate complex is probably failing to form during the reaction.

4. What if you add still more substrate to the mix and you find that it has no effect on the rate of enzyme activity? What would you now figure is happening?

A. The concentration of available enzyme has exceeded the concentration of substrate.
B. The concentration of available enzyme has exceeded the concentration of product.
C. The concentration of available enzyme has exceeded the concentration of enzyme-substrate complexes.
D. The concentration of substrate present has exceeded the concentration of available enzyme.

5. What is the term given for the situation described in question 4?

A. Saturation
B. Denaturation
C. Competition
D. Inhibition

GLOSSARY

active site
> the functional portion of an enzyme, where substrates bind

catalyst
> something that speeds up a chemical reaction but is not altered by the reaction

coenzyme
> helps an enzyme carry out its job; vitamins are coenzymes

denaturation
> the semipermanent disruption of bonds in a molecule; causes compounds such as enzymes or proteins to lose their shape and function

enzyme
> a type of protein that increases the rate of a reaction

enzyme-substrate complex
> a temporary structure produced when substrates bind to an enzyme; initiates the reaction

lock-and-key theory
> the idea that each enzyme's active site offers a precise fit for only one (usually) set of substrates, i.e., enzymes are not interchangeable—they are highly specific

optimal pH
> the pH at which an enzyme functions at its personal best; this differs depending on what enzyme we're talking about

product
> what's produced when a reaction occurs

reactants
> whatever is going to interact during a reaction to produce product

saturation point
> the point at which there are more substrate molecules than there are enzymes available to handle them

substrate
> what an enzyme does its job on when it speeds up the rate of a reaction; the substrate binds to the enzyme

x-axis
> horizontal axis of a graph

y-axis
> vertical axis of a graph

ANSWER KEY

Check Your Progress 1

1. D
2. rate
3. C

Check Your Progress 2

1. yes
2. no
3. yes
4. no
5. no
6. yes
7. yes
8. no

Check Your Progress 3

1. F
2. T
3. T
4. T

Check Your Progress 4

1. high or low pH; high temperature
2. low: slows down an enzyme; high: denatures bonds and cripples an enzyme
3. B
4. D
5. A

The Cell Membrane and Cellular Transport

There is a saying that no man is an island, meaning that a person cannot isolate himself from the rest of the world. In certain respects, however, the same cannot be said of a cell. Each cell acts as its own little island by carefully regulating what enters and leaves its premises. In order to see how the cell does this, we need to take a look at its ingenious line of defense, the *cell membrane.*

LIFE, AS IN BEAUTY, MAY BE ONLY SKIN-DEEP

Think of the cell membrane as the skin of a cell. Like our own skin, it acts as a protective barrier, helping to keep internal things inside and external things outside. This is incredibly important; can you imagine, for instance, the chaos that would result if your skin absorbed everything that surrounded you, or let your fluids and cells out willy-nilly? The results would be downright ugly, not to mention fatal to you as an organism. The cell membrane's job is to maintain the cell's integrity as a tiny, living organism in an extracellular world. That means keeping constant vigil over what enters and leaves the cell.

The cell membrane accomplishes this monumental task through its molecular structure. (We hope you didn't think that we were through with chemistry.) The cell membrane is made up of a *lipid bilayer*. If the word "lipid" rings a bell, that's good—it's the same class of compounds we talked about in Chapter 2. "Bilayer" means that we're talking about two layers here. This is how a lipid bilayer is assembled in a cell membrane:

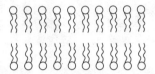

If these lipid molecules look to you like mirror images of each other, it's not a mirage—they really are arranged that way in a cell membrane. Which leads to the question—why?

It turns out that lipid molecules have two strikingly different parts within their structures. Each lipid molecule has a *hydrophobic* section and a *hydrophilic* section. The hydrophobic part avoids all water or water-like molecules. The hydrophilic part happens to seek out those very molecules.

FYI

Imagine thinking like a lipid for a moment. If your arms sought out one type of environment while your legs shunned the very same environment. Sounds like your body might go through some interesting convolutions.

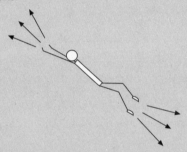

Well, the lipid molecule also acts out its dual interests: the hydrophilic section positions itself near water-like molecules and the hydrophobic section moves as far away from water-like molecules as it possibly can.

Now that you know a whole lot more about the lipid molecules that form the bilayer, let's take another look at that structure:

outside of cell

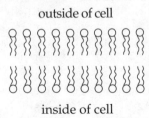

inside of cell

One side of the bilayer faces the outside of the cell (called the *extracellular space*), and the other side faces the inside of the cell. We want to tell you right now that both the inside and outside of the cell are aqueous (watery) in nature.

Now you're ready to take on this question:

In the lipid bilayer shown above, which piece of each lipid molecule is the hydrophilic piece, and which is the hydrophobic one?

The answer: The round part of each lipid molecule—called the *head*—is hydrophilic; it faces the aqueous surroundings both inside and outside of the cell. The squiggly pieces in each lipid molecule—called the *tail*—are hydrophobic, and they hide themselves within the center of the lipid molecule. This way they cleverly avoid exposing themselves to any aqueous environments.

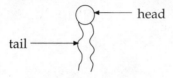

one lipid molecule

SOME PROTEINS RUN THROUGH IT— THE FLUID MOSAIC MODEL

When we told you that the cell membrane is made up of a lipid bilayer, we left something out. Lipids are not the only thing that makes up a cell membrane—proteins play a big role, too. The proteins fit into the lipid bilayer in more than one arrangement. Some span the entire membrane from one surface to the other, others sit on the outer part of the bilayer, and still others sit on the inner part of the bilayer.

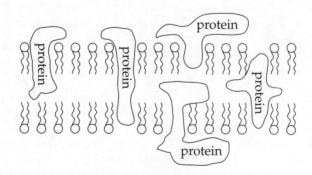

This arrangement—all of these proteins situated within or on the lipid bilayer—is called the *fluid mosaic model* of the cell membrane.

CHECK YOUR PROGRESS 1

1. The cell membrane is primarily composed of

   A. polysaccharides and proteins
   B. nucleic acids and polysaccharides
   C. lipids and carbohydrates
   D. lipids and proteins

2. A molecule that is hydrophobic will behave in which of the following ways when placed in an aqueous environment?

   A. It will attempt to minimize its contact with its surroundings.
   B. It will attempt to maximize its contact with its surroundings.
   C. It will disintegrate upon contact with its surroundings.
   D. It will form hydrogen bonds with atoms in its surroundings.

3. Which of the following pictures best depicts the arrangement that a handful of lipid molecules would take on when tossed into an aqueous environment?

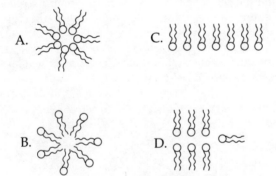

4. Dear valued customer,

Congratulations! Here is the fluid mosaic model of the cell membrane that you requested. Assembly is required, but glue is not. Snap off the molecules to construct your model. Questions or comments? Call Cells-R-Us at 1-800-The Cell.

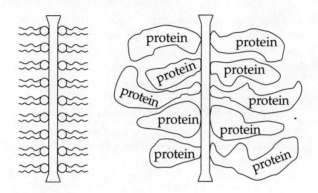

Assemble your model here:

CELL TRANSPORT

Now that we have all the necessary pieces of the cell membrane in place, let's see how they interact to allow some things to come and go—and to deny other things access. Three major forms of transport directly through the cell membrane are *diffusion, facilitated transport*, and *active transport*.

Diffusion

Little molecules can generally pass into and out of the cell membrane pretty easily. The cell membrane is sort of like an open door to these items, and they slip between the lipid molecules into or out of the cell. This is called diffusion.

It's a Breeze for a Cell to Conduct Diffusion

In diffusion, a substance is able to cross the cell membrane and the cell doesn't have to use up any of its energy to allow that to happen.

Since nothing in life is ever quite that simple, there are two conditions that must be met before diffusion can actually happen:

1. The cell membrane must be *permeable* to whatever small molecule is trying to pass through: it must present an opening specifically for that molecule.

The cell membrane decides on a substance-by-substance basis just what it will allow to pass through. Whatever it's not permeable to, doesn't gain access. After all, no one can pass through a door if the door is closed. For some substances, the lipid molecules act as an open door—and for others, the lipid molecules close rank and the door is shut tight. That's why biologists call the cell membrane a *semipermeable* membrane—it lets only some stuff pass through.

2. A substance can only move from an area that is *more* crowded with that substance to an area that is *less* crowded with the substance.

For instance, let's say that some amino acids want to move into a cell. They're small enough to get in, and the cell membrane is permeable to them. So far, so good. But, there has to be *more* amino acids on the outside of the cell and *less* amino acids on the inside of the cell in order for the amino acids to enter the cell by diffusion.

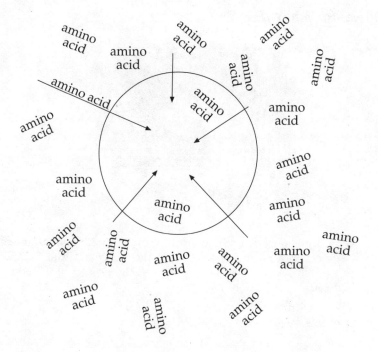

Likewise, if some amino acids want to leave the cell by diffusion, then there has to be more amino acids *inside* the cell than *outside* in order for that to happen.

When we talk about "amounts" of molecules, we're really discussing their *concentrations*.

A Diffusion Minireview

Let's do a minireview here. We'll just sort of think out loud about the major points we've covered on diffusion. (This kind of casual, brief review is a great way to solidify what you learn as you go along—try it yourself here and there throughout the book).

First Point—Diffusion doesn't require energy, and it takes place through a semipermeable membrane.

Second Point—Diffusion can only happen if there is a concentration gradient—that is, if there is a difference in the amount of the diffusing substance on one side of the membrane, compared to on the other side.

Third Point—A substance always diffuses from an area of higher concentration to one of lower concentration.

Osmosis Is a Form of Diffusion

Now that you know how diffusion works, we're going to tell you about a special form of diffusion called *osmosis*. Osmosis is the specific name given to the diffusion of water.

Let's say a cell is sitting in some extracellular fluid. Inside the cell are lots of organelles, along with many big molecules and ions and stuff. So there are a whole lot of items (called *solutes*) inside the cell. Outside the cell there aren't too many of these items; instead, there's a lot of liquid (called *solvent*).

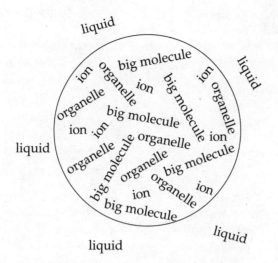

liquid

Since the cell is semipermeable (it lets some things across but not others), the big things in the cell can't get out, but the water molecules outside the cell can get in. The water molecules want to get in, in order to balance out the uneven ratio across the membrane between solutes and solvent. (Since the solutes can't get out, the solvent goes in.) The solvent's entrance into the cell membrane is by osmosis.

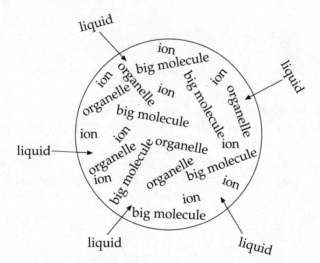

Of course, osmosis can also happen in the reverse direction. If the cell were placed in a surrounding that had more solutes in it than the cell had, then water would *leave* the cell by osmosis.

If all this doesn't immediately click into place, don't panic. You just have to give osmosis time to sink in. Read the explanation again, look up its definition from another source, draw out a couple of scenarios based on what we said above, and discover it for yourself at your own pace.

CHECK YOUR PROGRESS 2

Questions 1 and 2 refer to the following scenario:

There's a very small amount of salt (NaCl) inside a cell with a semipermeable membrane. Salt is able to pass through the membrane. There's a lot of salt outside of the cell. (Draw a picture for yourself now in the space below, and see how much easier it becomes to answer questions 1 and 2.)

Your picture:

1. Will salt diffuse out of the cell into the surroundings, or will it diffuse into the cell from the surroundings?

2. Is the transport of salt across the membrane a form of osmosis? Why or why not?

3. All of the following are true regarding diffusion across a cell membrane EXCEPT

   A. transport is from an area of higher concentration to one of lower concentration
   B. transport is through a semipermeable membrane
   C. transport does not require energy
   D. transport is against the concentration gradient

Facilitated Transport

What if a substance wants to leave the cell along its concentration gradient but the cell membrane is not permeable to the substance? Is there any way that the substance can get through in spite of the membrane's impermeability?

Maybe so—it turns out that for some substances, the proteins that are embedded within the cell membrane can help out. The proteins can somehow help the substance pass through the membrane, or even actually escort the substance through the membrane. This type of transport is called *facilitated transport,* because membrane-bound proteins help a substance to pass through the bilayer.

FYI

Facilitated transport doesn't require any energy from the cell. It still involves movement from an area of higher concentration to an area of lower concentration, only that movement is made possible by membrane proteins (hence the name "facilitated").

Active Transport

Everything we've discussed so far (diffusion, osmosis, and facilitated transport) has been a form of *passive transport*—they haven't required any energy in order to occur. Why not? Because transport was always in a direction from higher to lower concentration, and that's what nature favors.

Now let's consider what happens when transport is in a direction from *lower* to *higher* concentration. What if a substance needs, say, to enter the cell, but there's more of the substance inside the cell than there is outside the cell? The concentration gradient is all wrong for this to happen by simple or even facilitated diffusion. Does the cell have any other options if it really wants this substance inside? As a matter of fact, it does—it can opt for *active transport.*

In active transport, a substance can move across the cell membrane *against* its concentration gradient. (This *doesn't* follow the natural order of things in the universe; that's why it requires energy.)

Active transport is going to cost the cell some energy by using up some energy molecules called *ATP.* We'll be seeing a whole lot more of these molecules later on. For now, we just want you to know that the cell must supply some ATP any time that active transport takes place.

CAN YOU BELIEVE THE PROGRESS YOU'RE MAKING? IT'S ALREADY TIME FOR ANOTHER MINIREVIEW

Let's do a quick highlight of the different methods of transport across a cell membrane.

> *One—Diffusion.* Requires a semipermeable membrane; takes no energy; movement is from higher to lower concentration.
>
> *Two—Facilitated transport.* Requires help of proteins; takes no energy; movement is from higher to lower concentration.
>
> *Three—Active transport.* Requires a semipermeable membrane; takes energy; movement is from lower to higher concentration.

ENDOCYTOSIS AND EXOCYTOSIS

So far we've covered the ways in which substances pass directly through the cell membrane. There is another method by which some things can enter and leave the cell, though—*endocytosis* and *exocytosis*.

ENDOCYTOSIS—WHEN YOU'RE SURROUNDED ON ALL SIDES

What we're going to tell you almost sounds like science fiction, but it's not. For some substances, a section of the cell membrane actually surrounds the substance and then encloses it in a small membrane-bound pocket. In this way, the substance that was *outside* of the cell now finds itself *inside*. The way in which the cell membrane surrounds and engulfs something is called endocytosis.

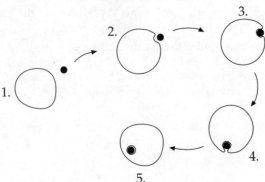

Pinocytosis and *phagocytosis* are both forms of endocytosis. In pinocytosis ("cell drinking") the cell membrane engulfs bits of liquid; in phagocytosis ("cell eating") the cell engulfs solid particles or bits of particles, which would have a hard time passing through the lipid bilayer.

Exocytosis

Things can get routed out of the cell via exocytosis. When the cell wants to get rid of something that's inside and enclosed in a vesicle (surrounded by a minimembrane), it sends the vesicle and its contents over to the cell membrane. The vesicle joins (*fuses* is the correct biological term) the cell membrane and in doing so, pops out its contents into the extracellular space. Voila—what was just inside the cell finds itself on the outside, in no uncertain terms. We're not going to pursue what happens to the contents once they are outside of the cell. We just wanted to cover how they got there.

CHECK YOUR PROGRESS 3

1. Which of the following is true with regard to facilitated transport?

    A. It is a passive process.
    B. It is an active process.
    C. It operates against a concentration gradient.
    D. It requires ATP in order to operate.

2. List the name of the cell membrane components that play a direct role in facilitated transport:

    _____ .

For questions 3 through 5, answer "yes" or "no" as you see fit.

3. Does active transport require energy? _____

4. Does active transport operate along (or down) a concentration gradient? _____

5. If there are more amino acids inside of a cell than outside, and amino acids leave the cell, do they leave by active transport? _____

6. What process is taking place in the picture directly below?

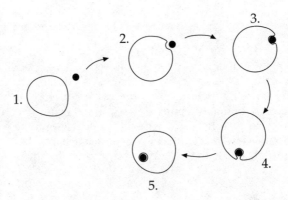

A. Active transport
B. Osmosis
C. Facilitated transport
D. Endocytosis

Questions 7 and 8 refer to the following scenario:

Someone reliable went through the trouble of quantifying the relative amounts of a few items found inside, and directly outside, of a certain cell. The results are listed below. This same person also worked late into the night to determine that the cell membrane was permeable to items B and Z but not to items A or X.

Items found *inside* the cell	Items found *outside* the cell
A (16 units)	A (4,000 units)
B (200 units)	B (4 units)
X (1,200 units)	X (0 units)
Z (.006 units)	Z (744 units)

7. Which item(s) will enter the cell by diffusion?

   A. A only
   B. Z only
   C. A and Z only
   D. A, B, and Z

8. Which item(s) can exit the cell by active transport?

   A. B only
   B. Z only
   C. X only
   D. B and Z only

9. Pinocytosis is a term applied to

   A. a form of phagocytosis
   B. a type of adolescent angst
   C. a segment of the cell membrane
   D. a form of exocytosis

GLOSSARY

active transport

movement from a region of lower concentration to a region of higher concentration; because it is against the concentration gradient, it requires energy

ATP

a molecule that acts as a source of energy in the cell; its true name is adenosine triphosphate

concentration gradient

a difference in concentration of an item across a given area; for instance, if there were more salt outside a cell than inside, then a concentration gradient would exist for salt in that area. On the other hand, if there were the same amount of salt inside and outside of the cell, then no concentration gradient would exist for salt.

diffusion

a passive form of transport across a semipermeable barrier; the direction is from an area of higher to lower concentration, and the membrane must be permeable to the diffusing substance

endocytosis

a process in which a segment of the cell membrane surrounds a particle and encloses it within a vesicle, thereby transporting it from the outside of the cell to the inside

exocytosis

a vesicle and its contents are transported from the interior of the cell to the cell membrane, where the vesicle fuses with the lipid bilayer and releases its contents into the extracellular space

facilitated transport

a passive form of transport across a cell membrane made possible by the assistance of membrane-bound proteins

fluid mosaic model

a model of the cell membrane that depicts the structure as a lipid bilayer with proteins interspersed throughout the exterior, the interior, and spanning the bilayer

hydrophilic

a tendency to be drawn to water molecules

hydrophobic

a tendency to avoid water molecules

lipid bilayer

the structural arrangement of the lipid molecules of a cell membrane; consists of a double layer of lipid molecules with hydrophobic tails pointed inwards towards each other and hydrophilic heads pointed outwards towards the extracellular space at one face and the interior of the cell at the other

osmosis

a specific form of diffusion involving the passive movement of water

passive transport

transport of a substance across a semipermeable membrane; does not require energy, because movement is from a region of higher concentration to one of lower concentration

permeable

access across a barrier (such as a membrane) for a given substance

phagocytosis

"cell eating"; a form of endocytosis for large particles

pinocytosis

"cell drinking"; a form of endocytosis for liquid particles

semipermeable membrane

a membrane that acts as a barrier for certain substances but allows other substances to pass through it

solute

something that gets dissolved in a solution (e.g., in a solution of saltwater, salt is the solute)

solvent

some type of liquid that permits a solute to exist in it (e.g., in a solution of saltwater, water is the solvent)

ANSWER KEY

Check Your Progress 1

1. D

2. A

3. B

4.

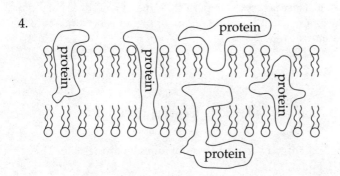

Check Your Progress 2

1. salt will diffuse into the cell from the surroundings

2. no, because osmosis only refers to the diffusion of water across a semipermeable membrane

3. D

Check Your Progress 3

1. A

2. proteins

3. yes

4. no

5. no

6. D

7. B

8. A

9. A

5

The Cell and Its Organelles

SOLD ON CELLS

Why do biology books always make such a big deal out of cells? Well, in case you haven't put it together yet, cells are the most basic living unit of all living things. And biology is the study of living things. If cells weren't around, *we* wouldn't be around. And neither would biology. (We suspect that you have a few comments of your own to add right here.)

CELL ORGANELLES

Our bodies have organs that carry out specific functions. Zoom in a little closer and you'll find that each one of our cells has *organelles* to perform specific jobs. We mentioned that a cell is the smallest living unit. Cellular organelles are substructures of a cell; they are not alive. In this chapter, we're going to zero in on these cellular organelles and find out just what it is they do.

Live from Hollywood

You're already practically an expert on one organelle—the plasma membrane—from reading chapter 4. Now, thanks to the modern wonders of satellite, we're going to take a moment to meet some other famous organelles of the cell. Keep in mind during the show that, since a *cell* is microscopic in size, the organelles found *within* it certainly are, too.

Setting: A stage with a runway attached, surrounded by seating that is filled to capacity. An announcer is on stage holding a microphone.

Announcer: "And now—(drum roll)—it gives me great pleasure to introduce to you on this page—direct from an animal cell in Hollywood—(pause)—the cellular organelles!"

(sound of heavy applause)

"Let's give a big hand to. . .

. . .the mitochondria!" *(to sound of applause):*

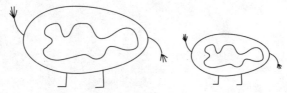

. . .the nucleus!" *(to sound of cheering):*

. . .the nucleolus!" *(to sound of whistling):*

. . .the cytoplasm!" *(to sound of cat calls):*

. . .the lysosomes!" *(to sound of cheering):*

. . .the peroxisomes!" *(to sound of hooting):*

. . .the endoplasmic reticulum!" *(to sound of polite clapping):*

...the Golgi apparatus!" *(to sound of applause):*

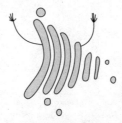

...the ribosomes!" *(to sound of whistling):*

...the centrioles!" *(to sound of cat calls):*

...and last, but not least...the vacuoles!" *(to applause at a deafening roar):*

Don't worry if you didn't recognize any of these subcellular celebrities. By the end of this chapter, you'll know intimate details of their lives.

THE ROAD TRIP HOME

After a harrowing road trip home in a converted school bus, during which the cytoplasm had to be scraped up off the bus floorboards, the nucleus' chromosomes nearly unraveled, and the lysosomes almost lost their hydrolytic enzymes, the organelles made it safely back home, to their animal cell.

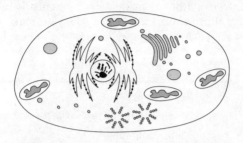

A normal animal cell, with its organelles where they belong.

THE SCOOP ON EACH ORGANELLE

You heard it here first, an exclusive on each organelle's lifestyle.

MITOCHONDRIA

While some things are accused of being thick-skinned, we've never heard of something being called double-skinned. But that's just what a mitochondrion has—a double membrane. Pick out any mitochondrion in a cell and it will have both an *inner membrane* and an *outer membrane*.

The inner membrane is not your usual straightforward one, either. Instead it twists and turns like a miniature roller coaster track. Now let's think about this: a membrane that crests and dips periodically has a lot of extra surface area. What's all that surface area needed for? The answer has to do with the mitochondrion's job: Mitochondria manufacture energy for the cell. In other words, they produce ATP.

All that surface area provided by the inner folds of the mitochondrial membrane allows the mitochondria to supply the cell with lots of ATP. (You'll find out how in chapter 6.)

Food for Thought

Do you think that a very active muscle cell (which needs a lot of energy) would contain more or less mitochondria than would a quieter type of cell? If you said "more," you're right. The muscle cell, which does a lot of energy-requiring contracting, contains many more mitochondria than does, say, an adipocyte (fat cell).

The Nucleus

Somewhere near the center of most cells is a large, easy-to-spot roundish organelle. That's the nucleus. The nucleus is enclosed by a double membrane called the *nuclear envelope*.

What is the nucleus' job? Think of the nucleus as the central control panel of the cell. This powerful little organelle determines nearly all of what goes on in a cell. Like, "crank up production of a certain protein," or "stop making enzyme Y for awhile." Whatever the cell's activity, the nucleus rules it.

FYI

Why should the nucleus be in charge?

Because it contains all of the *chromosomes* of the cell.

And the chromosomes contain *DNA*.

And DNA contains *genes*.

And genes direct the *activities* of a cell.

(You'll learn all about chromosomes, DNA, and genes in chapter 8.)

Once again: the nucleus is in charge of the cell, and that's because it contains chromosomes, which contain DNA.

The Nucleolus

It's not an accident that the nucleolus is spelled a lot like "nucleus." Look for the nucleus of a cell and you'll also spot the nucleolus. That's because the nucleolus is actually a dense section that lies within the nucleus. Under a microscope, it kind of looks like a stain on a rug, but don't try to describe it that way on an exam.

What does the nucleolus do? It produces ribosomes.

Another word for ribosomes is *ribosomal RNA*, or *rRNA* for short. So the nucleolus manufactures ribosomes, and sends them out of the nucleus and into the cytoplasm to form functional ribosomes. It can be said that most of the ribosome is made in the nucleolus.

The Cytoplasm

Touch a peeled grape and you'll have a fair idea of the consistency and feel of cytoplasm. It's sort of wet and gel-like, it's got some form but it's also rather fluid. Where is it? It's found throughout the cell and it's bordered by the plasma membrane on one side and the nuclear membrane on the other.

The cytoplasm is a happening place. A relative lack of structure does not mean a lack of function. Lots of things happen in the cytoplasm, like a sort of intracellular circulation called *cytoplasmic streaming*, diffusion, transport, and many biochemical reactions. The cytoplasm also serves as the medium in which all the other organelles hang out.

Check Your Progress 1

For questions 1-7, choose from among the answer choices provided below.

    A. Nucleus
    B. Nucleolus
    C. Mitochondrion
    D. Cytoplasm

1. Produces ribosomes

2. Spans the cell between the nuclear envelope and the cell membrane

3. Controls all activities of the cell

4. Located within the nucleus

5. Double-membraned; site of ATP production

6. Serves as a medium for other organelles; site of numerous biochemical reactions

7. Contains DNA in the form of chromosomes

The Lysosomes

Lysosomes are small, membrane-bound sac-like structures that contain digestive enzymes. The membrane keeps these *hydrolytic* (as in "hydrolysis," from chapter 3) enzymes enclosed and away from the rest of the cell. So what are these enzymes' targets? Any old, worn out bits and pieces of the cell, debris, and ingested stuff. The enzymes chew up these things inside the lysosome. Now let's rephrase that in proper biological terms:

Lysosomes contain hydrolytic enzymes that digest wastes and ingested materials.

FYI

At least one autoimmune disease—*rheumatoid arthritis*—is suspected to be caused in part by leaky lysosomes. These lysosomes let some of their hydrolytic enzymes loose to wreak havoc on cartilage cells in the joints.

THE PEROXISOMES

Like lysosomes, peroxisomes are small, membrane-bound sac-like structures. And also like lysosomes, they contain enzymes. So what makes them peroxisomes instead of lysosomes? This does:

Peroxisomes contain *catalases*, a type of enzyme that breaks down destructive hydrogen peroxide into harmless water and oxygen.

THE ENDOPLASMIC RETICULUM

We have just one word for you concerning this extensive organelle, and that word is "membrane." The endoplasmic reticulum (ER for short) is made up of a series of connected membrane sheets that originate off the nuclear envelope, and winds its way throughout the cytoplasm.

Now, what does this intriguing organelle do? For starters, it contains a variety of enzymes that catalyze all sorts of different reactions. But what you mainly need to know about it is:

The endoplasmic reticulum produces, transports, and stores proteins.

ROUGH VS. SMOOTH ER

A quirk of the endoplasmic reticulum is that it consists of two types:

Rough ER—Just like it sounds—bumps on the RER show up as small black dots on the membrane. These small black dots are ribosomes. Since ribosomes make protein, and rough ER contains ribosomes, then rough ER also serves as a location for protein synthesis. Remember that.

Smooth ER—You guessed it—SER is just endoplasmic reticulum minus the bumps. Not all ER has ribosomes on its membrane face. Since SER doesn't contain ribosomes, it obviously isn't involved in protein synthesis.

THE GOLGI APPARATUS
(A.K.A. GOLGI COMPLEX AND GOLGI BODY)

Wherever the endoplasmic reticulum is, the Golgi apparatus won't be far away. That's because proteins made on the rough ER get sent to the Golgi apparatus for further processing.

Like the ER, the Golgi apparatus also consists of a series of membranes, but in this case the membranes are flattened and unconnected. They're compressed near one another in a parallel fashion. Also associated with this organelle are small vesicles (little membrane-bound circles).

The Golgi apparatus has two functions

1. It packages things, like proteins that are going to be sent out of the cell.

"One Protein Molecule—To Go, Please"

What in the world do we mean by "packaging?" Certainly not a gift box with a ribbon. Packaging a protein means modifying it in some way, like sticking a bunch of carbohydrate molecules on it.

---

2. It transports these products to the cell membrane so they can be secreted. (That's why the Golgi apparatus is conveniently located between the ER and the cell membrane.) The idea is that little vesicles filled with the secretory protein break off the Golgi and head over to the cell membrane. They then fuse with the cell membrane and dump their secretory protein outside the cell.

CHECK YOUR PROGRESS 2

For questions 1-7, choose from among the four answer choices provided below.

   A. Lysosomes
   B. Peroxisomes
   C. Endoplasmic reticulum
   D. Golgi apparatus

1. Consists of extensive sheets of connected membrane

2. Single-membraned; contain catalases

3. Small and sac-like; degrade worn out structures and foreign matter

4. Modifies, packages, and transports secretory proteins

5. Degrade hydrogen peroxide into water and oxygen

6. Its "rough" sections are the sites of protein synthesis

7. Contain hydrolytic enzymes

THE RIBOSOMES

Ribosomes have already cropped up here and there, like under "the nucleolus," and "the endoplasmic reticulum." Well, here they get their own spotlight. A ribosome is made from RNA, a molecule you'll get to know better in chapter 8. A ribosome has two subunits: a larger one and a smaller one. Big and little. When the ribosome is not being depicted as a little black dot, it's depicted sort of like a chef's hat.

Now a ribosome by any other name would still produce proteins, because that's its job. A ribosome is this "place" where proteins get made. In proper biological terms, ribosomes are the sites of protein synthesis.

THE CENTRIOLES (SHORT AND SWEET)

Little needs to be said about centrioles. Basically, they're these cylindrical organelles that hang out in pairs in the cell. What are they made of? Protein-derived structures called *microtubules.* What do they do? They function in cell division.

And another thing: Just before cell division, two pairs of centrioles are present. During cell division, one pair goes to each daughter cell.

THE VACUOLES

It's not much of a leap when you see the term "vacuole" to conjure up the word "vacuum" (not the Hoover model, but as in Latin, for "empty space"). A vacuole is simply an empty space that's surrounded by a single membrane. There are lots of different types of vacuoles in a cell. Some store water; others store food; still others store other stuff.

THE CONTRACTILE VACUOLE: A PROTOZOAN'S AUTO-EJECTOR

One important vacuole to know about is the *contractile vacuole* of protozoans. A protozoan is a single-celled organism (examples are the *Euglena* and the *Paramecium*). Now think about this for a second: here are these organisms that consist entirely of one—singular—cell. Compare that to humans, who slough off or otherwise dispose of scores of cells every day, without even noticing!

When a protozoan's contractile vacuole fills with water, it contracts, expelling its contents out of the cell. So the contractile vacuole's job is to fling water out of the cell. In biospeak, that means it functions in maintaining the protozoan's water balance with its environment.

CHECK YOUR PROGRESS 3

For questions 1-8, choose from among the answers provided below.

    A. Ribosomes
    B. Centrioles
    C. Vacuoles
    D. Contractile vacuole

1. May be filled with water, food, or other storage items

2. Function as the sites of protein synthesis

3. Function in cell division

4. Spaces surrounded by a single membrane

5. Composed of RNA

6. Made from protein-derived microtubules

7. May exist in free or in bound states

8. Found in protozoans; helps to maintain water balance

A FEW ODDS AND ENDS

The cell has a few other structures that you need to remember.

MICROFILAMENTS

Riddle: What's long and thin and made of one kind of protein?

Answer: Microfilaments

Microfilaments are a type of fiber that help to give a cell some shape and form. For that reason, they help to make up the cell's *cytoskeleton* (a cell's equivalent to our bones). Microfilaments also help the cell to move around (in other words, they assist in motility).

MICROTUBULES

Riddle: What's long and hollow and made of another kind of protein?

Answer: Microtubules

Microtubules are a type of stiff fiber that also give a cell structure. So, like microfilaments, microtubules are a component of the cytoskeleton. Microtubules also get together in bundles to create *cilia* and *flagella*. What are they? We're glad you asked.

CILIA AND FLAGELLA

Some cells have either many cilia or one or two flagella to help them move around (that's *motility* in proper bio terms). A cilium is a short, hair-like structure on the cell membrane that moves in a stroke-like fashion, like an oar would. A flagellum, on the other hand, is a long, whip-like structure that moves in a whip-like motion.

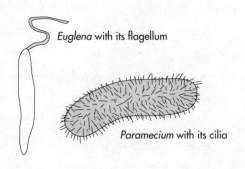

Euglena with its flagellum

Paramecium with its cilia

Plenty of human cells make use of cilia or flagella. Cells in your airway, for instance, have lots of cilia to clear little bits of debris out of the air passages, sort of like those sweeping street cleaners you see around (but much more effectual, unless you smoke). Cells in the fallopian tubes have cilia to help push the egg toward the uterus. Sperm cells, on the other hand, each have a flagellum to propel them toward the egg cell.

Many protozoans also possess either cilia or a flagellum so they can get around. For instance, the *Euglena* has a single flagellum, and the *Paramecium* has so many cilia that it resembles a plush rug under the scanning electron microscope.

PROKARYOTIC CELLS VS. EUKARYOTIC CELLS

Here's how you can tell a *prokaryotic* cell from a *eukaryotic* one: ask yourself, "Does it have a membrane around its nucleus?" If the answer is "yes," it's a eukaryote. If the answer's "no," then it's a prokaryote.

PROKARYOTIC CELLS

Prokaryotic cells are simpler than eukaryotic cells. They lack a lot of structures that eukaryotes have. For instance, a prokaryote has no nuclear membrane. What else is it missing? Arranged chromosomes (the DNA is loosely organized, instead), mitochondria, ER, Golgi apparatus, and many other structures.

Bacteria are Prokaryotes

Bacteria are made up of one cell, and come in an assortment of shapes. Round, pea-shaped ones are called *cocci* (one is a *coccus*). Rod-shaped ones, like Good and Plenty candy, are called *bacilli* (one is a *bacillus*). Corkscrew-shaped ones, like. . .well. . .a corkscrew, are called *spirilla* (one is a *spirillum*).

Because bacteria are prokaryotes, they're missing all the stuff listed above. What they *do* have, though, is a *cell wall.* That cell wall is a bacterium's Achilles heel when bacteria infect humans. Have you ever wondered why taking an antibiotic such as penicillin will help you to get rid of an infection? Well, here's why: antibiotics disable bacteria. They put them out of commission, stop the party. The penicillin targets the bacterial cell wall, and since human cells don't have a cell wall, they're protected from its action.

FYI

Why won't penicillin work on a virus? While an antibiotic like penicillin generally works well on bacteria, all the penicillin in the world won't disable a *virus.* That's because a virus *has no* cell wall to tamper with. It doesn't have many other potential targets either. A virus is made of only two things: a *protein coat* on the outside, and a piece of DNA or RNA on the inside to program things.

Even though a virus travels light, it's highly capable of infecting humans. It simply injects its DNA or RNA into a human's cell and that piece of DNA or RNA forces the human cell to use its own equipment to produce a whole bunch of little new viruses. These infect more human cells nearby. The virus' apparent immunity from attack is what makes the AIDS virus, for instance, so devastating.

EUKARYOTIC CELLS

Most cells are eukaryotic. A eukaryotic cell does have a nuclear membrane. It also comes with everything that's missing in prokaryotes: arranged chromosomes, mitochondria, etc.

Check Your Progress 4

1. Which is the more primitive cell, a eukaryote, or a prokaryote? _____.

2. A botanist is examining a cell she plucked from the waters of a nearby pond. Viewing it under a microscope, she is able to identify a nucleus. The nucleus is not surrounded by a nuclear membrane, nor is its DNA arranged in an organized fashion. Based on these observations, she would characterize the cell as a [prokaryote ___ eukaryote ___].

3. Which of the following structures does NOT exist in both eukaryotic and prokaryotic cells?
   A. Cell membrane
   B. Nucleus
   C. DNA
   D. Mitochondria

4. Bacteria are single-celled organisms that lack many structures found in other cells, such as microfilaments and microtubules, the Golgi apparatus, and an endoplasmic reticulum. Based on this information, bacteria most likely also:
   A. lack a nuclear envelope and are prokaryotic
   B. lack a nuclear membrane and are eukaryotic
   C. possess a nuclear membrane and are prokaryotic
   D. possess a nuclear membrane and are eukaryotic

GLOSSARY

bacilli

rod-shaped bacteria

bacteria

single-celled prokaryotic organisms containing a cell wall

catalase

an enzyme that breaks hydrogen peroxide into water and oxygen; found in peroxisomes

centrioles

exist as pairs in a cell; function in cell division; made up of microtubules

chromosomes

structures found in the cell nucleus; composed of protein and DNA

cilia

short, hair-like structures made up of microtubules; allow a cell to move; motion is an oar-like stroke

cocci

round-shaped bacteria

contractile vacuole

a vacuole that regulates water balance in protozoa; it ejects water from the cell

cytoplasm

gel-like substance in which most of the organelles reside; site of many biochemical reactions

cytoskeleton

composed mainly of microfilaments and microtubules; give a cell form and structure

DNA

found in the nucleus in the form of chromosomes; contains genes

endoplasmic reticulum

a series of connected membranes within the cell that produce, transport, and store secretory proteins

eukaryote

an organism whose cell(s) contain a nuclear membrane, along with many other structures, organized DNA, mitochondria, ER, Golgi apparatus, microfilaments and microtubules

flagellum

long, whip-like structure made up of microtubules; allows a cell to move; motion is whip-like

gene
a segment of DNA that codes for production of a specific product

Golgi apparatus
a series of flattened membranes that store, modify, and transport secretory proteins

hydrolytic enzymes
found in lysosomes; degrade old, worn-out materials

lysosomes
single-membraned sac-like organelles filled with hydrolytic enzymes

microfilaments
long, thin fibers that give a cell shape, form, and/or motility; part of cytoskeleton

microtubules
stiff, hollow fibers that give a cell shape, form, and/or motility; part of cytoskeleton

mitochondria
double-membraned organelles; produce ATP

nucleolus
organelle found within the nucleus; produces ribosomes

nucleus
round-shaped structure near center of cell; controls all cellular activities; contains DNA

penicillin
an antibiotic that targets the bacterial cell wall during a bacterial infection

peroxisome
sac-like organelles; their single membrane encloses hydrolytic enzymes that degrade worn-out cell parts

prokaryote
an organism whose nucleus lacks a nuclear membrane; many other organelles are also absent; it is more primitive than a eukaryote; bacteria are prokaryotes

protozoan
a single-celled (unicellular) organism; examples are the *Euglena* and *Paramecium*

ribosomes
made from RNA; sites of protein synthesis

rough ER
endoplasmic reticulum with ribosomes; site of protein synthesis

smooth ER

    endoplasmic reticulum without ribosomes

spirilli

    corkscrew-shaped bacteria

vacuole

    a subcellular space surrounded by a single membrane; often stores material

vesicle

    a very tiny space surrounded by a single membrane; often forms by breaking off from a larger membrane portion

virus

    not a cell, and no one's even sure whether it is a living or nonliving thing; composed only of a protein exterior and an inner segment of nucleic acid, either DNA or RNA

ANSWER KEY

Check Your Progress 1

1. B
2. D
3. A
4. B
5. C
6. D
7. A

Check Your Progress 2

1. C
2. B
3. A
4. D
5. B
6. C
7. A

Check Your Progress 3

1. C
2. A
3. B
4. C
5. A
6. B
7. A
8. D

Check Your Progress 4

1. prokaryote
2. prokaryote
3. D
4. A

CHAPTER 6

Cellular Respiration

THE CHICKEN AND THE EGG

We told you that the cell makes high-energy ATP molecules to fuel many of its activities. But where does the cell get the original energy that's used to make the ATP?

There is an answer to this riddle: the cell's original energy source is *glucose*. In *cellular respiration,* a cell breaks down glucose molecules and uses the energy that was locked up in the glucose molecules to make ATP.

WHAT IS GLYCOLYSIS?

Take a look at this word: *glycolysis*. That's glyco (as in "glucose") and lysis (as in "to break apart"). Now whenever you see this intimidating-looking word, you will immediately recognize that it names the biochemical process in which glucose is broken down.

Let's zero in on one little cell. More specifically, we'll be looking at the cell's cytoplasm, where glycolysis takes place.

$$\text{1 Glucose} \xrightarrow{\text{glycolysis}} \text{2 pyruvic acid}$$

So in glycolysis, 1 glucose molecule gets broken down into 2 *pyruvic acid* molecules.

FYI

Don't be surprised if you see the word "pyruvate" instead of "pyruvic acid." They both mean the same thing.

Anything else about glycolysis? Yes. The cell needs to supply 2 ATP to the process, but it gets a total of 4 ATP at the end. Final tally: for each glucose molecule, glycolysis yields 2 new ATP molecules.

Now you know glycolysis. (Of course, we've skipped all of the intermediate steps in the process in order to present it to you so neatly, but that's okay. We have to leave some things for when you get to college.)

WHAT HAPPENS TO THE PYRUVATE?

So the cell has performed glycolysis on one glucose molecule, and it has gained 2 extra ATP molecules. It also has 2 molecules of pyruvic acid as the end product of glycolysis. What does it do with the pyruvic acid molecules? Well, it turns out that there's still loads of energy locked up in them—energy that the cell wants. So the cell keeps working on the pyruvic acid molecules. In the next phase of molecular manipulation, the cell sends the 2 pyruvic acid molecules over to the mitochondria. There the 2 pyruvate are converted to 2 *acetyl CoA* molecules. Now the acetyl CoA molecules are ready to enter the *Krebs cycle*.

CHECK YOUR PROGRESS 1

1. Glycolysis is a process that breaks 1 glucose molecule down into 2 _____ _____ molecules.

2. How many net ATP molecules are produced when 1 molecule of glucose is broken down via glycolysis? _____

3. How many ATP molecules are used in the breakdown of 1 glucose molecule during glycolysis?

   _____

4. Which of the following is true regarding pyruvic acid?

   A. It contains little if any potential energy in its structure.
   B. It contains less energy than does glucose.
   C. It is created from acetyl CoA.
   D. It is formed in the mitochondria.

THE KREBS CYCLE

The Krebs cycle is also located in the mitochondria, where all the rest of the reactions will take place. Whenever you see this:

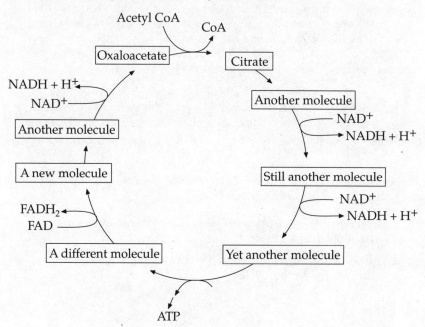

you're looking at the Krebs cycle (a.k.a. the *citric acid cycle*). Each acetyl CoA enters the Krebs cycle one molecule at a time. It joins up with *oxaloacetate* to gain entrance as *citrate*.

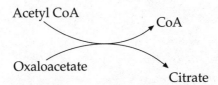

Think of it this way: you (acetyl CoA) arrive at a dance club (the Krebs cycle) and find out at the door that you can only get in as a couple. So you join up with the person hanging out at the entrance (oxaloacetate). Now you're not a single (acetyl CoA) anymore—you're a couple (citrate), so you're allowed to enter the dance club (the Krebs cycle).

Once in the Krebs cycle, the citrate quickly becomes transformed into something else and undergoes a bunch of further reactions. By the end of the cycle, however, oxaloacetate becomes available once again. It's as though the original couple that gained entrance (citric acid) doesn't exist anymore, and the person who arrived at the dance (acetyl CoA) is long gone, but the person who was hanging out at the entrance is back again, available for the next single (acetyl CoA) who arrives at the door. The oxaloacetate is available once again to join up with a new acetyl CoA for a spin around the Krebs cycle.

FYI

When we say that acetyl CoA enters the Krebs cycle, we mean that it enters as citrate and the citrate then undergoes a series of biochemical reactions that keep transforming it into different compounds. Those reactions happen in the mitochondrion because that's where the enzymes that catalyze those reactions are located.

The reactions that make up the Krebs cycle are often depicted as one big circle in order to emphasize the fact that the oxaloacetate molecule the acetyl CoA initially joined up with becomes available once again by the end of the cycle.

Here's a little recap of Krebs cycle events, because we know it takes a few rounds in order to become familiar:

1. acetyl CoA joins up with oxaloacetate and enters the Krebs cycle as citrate

2. all sorts of things happen to the citrate and its successors during the Krebs cycle

3. at the end of the cycle, oxaloacetate emerges once again

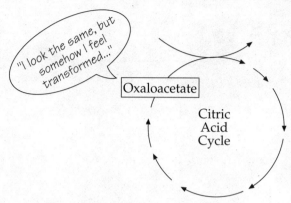

A MILLION-DOLLAR QUESTION

If what you start with is what you end up with, then what is the point of the Krebs cycle?

This: it generates an ATP, but more importantly, it pulls hydrogens and electrons off of the molecules that are going for a spin. It sticks those hydrogens and electrons onto something else (called NAD⁺ and FAD), so that these new molecules harbor lots of potential energy. These new molecules are called $FADH_2$ and NADH, and they promptly get shifted to the mitochondrion's inner membrane.

LEO Goes GER

Let's take a moment to look at oxidation and reduction, because it so happens that the crux of cellular respiration is all about oxidizing glucose and its successor molecules as far as the cell can push it.

- *In oxidation, a molecule loses an electron. That's LEO: Loss of Electron is Oxidation.*
- *In reduction, a molecule gains an electron. That's GER: Gain of Electron is Reduction.*
- *NAD⁺ is a coenzyme that takes on electrons. Its reduced form is NADH.*
- *FAD is another coenzyme that takes on electrons. Its reduced form is $FADH_2$.*

CHECK YOUR PROGRESS 2

1. The Krebs cycle takes place in the _____

   _____ .

2. Which one of the following molecules joins up
   with oxaloacetate and enters the Krebs cycle?

   A. Pyruvate
   B. Glucose
   C. Citrate
   D. Acetyl CoA

3. Which one of the following molecules remains once
   one complete turn of the Krebs cycle has occurred?

   A. Acetyl CoA
   B. Oxaloacetate
   C. Citrate
   D. Pyruvate

4. Which of the following get generated by the Krebs
   cycle?

   A. NAD$^+$ and FAD
   B. NADH and FADH$_2$
   C. ADP and inorganic phosphate
   D. H$_2$O

5. Another name for the Krebs cycle is the _____

   _____ .

6. The breakdown of 1 glucose molecule by glycolysis
   would result in how many turns of the Krebs
   cycle?

   A. 1
   B. 2
   C. 3
   D. 4

THE ELECTRON TRANSPORT CHAIN

Remember when we told you that the mitochondria make nearly all of a cell's ATP? Well, they need FADH$_2$ and NADH in order to do so. Here's what happens.

The Set-up: Sitting on all of that extra surface area of the inner mitochondrial membrane is the *electron transport chain.* Don't let the name intimidate you. If we said, "sitting on the inner mitochondrial membrane is an assortment of blackbirds," you wouldn't be phased. The electron transport chain is simply some different carrier molecules sitting near one another. (They have names like *ubiquinone* and *cytochrome b.*)

The Action: Electrons from our NADH and FADH$_2$ get passed down this chain—"handed," so to speak, from carrier to carrier down the line. Since the electrons are first given and then passed on to each successive carrier, the electron transport chain is essentially a series of oxidation-reduction (or *redox*) reactions. As electrons get handed from carrier molecule to carrier molecule, they give up a little energy at each point along the way.

The End of the Line

At the end of the carrier molecule chain, an oxygen awaits. The electrons get handed to the oxygen and water forms.

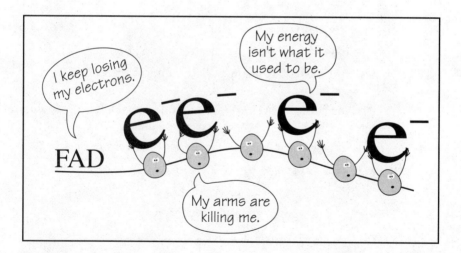

OXIDATIVE PHOSPHORYLATION

Here's where *oxidative phosphorylation* comes in. OP makes clever use of a proton concentration gradient to get its work done. As the NADH and FADH$_2$ are losing their electrons on the electron transport chain, they also lose their *protons.* The small increments of energy that get released as the electrons are passed from carrier to carrier get used to pump the protons right out of the *mitochondrial matrix* (the innermost part of the mitochondria). By establishing this proton gradient, the mitochondrion sets up some potential energy for it to tap into.

The Set-up: In certain spots on the inner mitochondrial membrane are special openings, or channels. Situated at these channels like ticket-takers are certain enzymes. These enzymes (like all enzymes) do one specific thing, and they do it well.

The Action: The protons that were pumped out of the matrix can only get back in one way: through the special channels on the inner mitochondrial membrane. Because there are more protons outside the matrix than inside, every time a proton enters the matrix through that opening some energy becomes available. And an enzyme sitting at that opening snaps up that energy and uses it to add a phosphate onto an ADP (adenosine diphosphate) molecule. Vóila—the mitochondrion has made some ATP.

BACKTRACKING

Because we just threw a whole lot of information at you, let's do a little backtracking to keep things straight.

The mitochondria made ATP.

It got its source of energy from the movement of protons down a concentration gradient.

The protons came from the electron transport chain.

The electron transport chain pulled them off of NADH and $FADH_2$.

The NADH and the $FADH_2$ were generated by the Krebs cycle.

Citric acid was the starting molecule for the Krebs cycle.

It came from acetyl CoA and oxaloacetate.

The acetyl CoA came from pyruvate.

The pyruvate was created via glycolysis.

Glycolysis broke down a glucose molecule.

There you have it—aerobic cellular respiration—forwards and backwards. Look over this whole section a few times and then construct the sequence of events your own way.

CHECK YOUR PROGRESS 3

1. The electron transport chain transports

   A. fuel
   B. spices
   C. electrons
   D. gold

2. An array of carrier molecules located on the _____ _____ make up the electron transport chain.

3. Each time an electron is passed from one carrier molecule to the next, some _____ is released.

4. In oxidative phosphorylation, a _____ gradient is established which ultimately provides energy for ADP and phosphate to join up to become _____ .

5. Where does the cell get the energy to pump protons generated by the electron transport chain outside of the mitochondrial matrix?

   A. From energy released when electrons are handed down the electron transport chain
   B. From ATP generated by the process of glycolysis
   C. From the conversion of pyruvate to acetyl CoA prior to when it enters the Krebs cycle
   D. From an ATP source located outside the cell

6. Which of the following species serves as the final hydrogen/electron acceptor in the electron transport chain?

   A. Hydrogen
   B. Nitrogen
   C. Oxygen
   D. Carbon

Aerobic vs. Anaerobic Respiration

With the exception of glycolysis, everything we've just covered is called *aerobic respiration* (it requires oxygen). Specifically, the Krebs cycle, the electron transport chain, and oxidative phosphorylation are all aerobic processes. Aerobic respiration is extremely efficient, squeezing out as much ATP as it can from a molecule of glucose. Overall, aerobic respiration yields 38 molecules of ATP per glucose. Organisms that conduct aerobic respiration (like us) are called *aerobes*.

Anaerobic respiration, on the other hand, is not very efficient. But don't tell that to the bacteria, yeast and muscle cells that engage in it. How is anaerobic respiration different from aerobic respiration? Well, it doesn't use oxygen at all. Anaerobic respiration starts out the same as aerobic respiration—with the process of glycolysis, which is anaerobic. We told you that glycolysis yields the cell a net of 2 ATP. Well, that's all that any cell that engages in anaerobic respiration gets—2 ATP. Compare that to 38 ATP for aerobic respiration, and you see why we say it's comparatively inefficient. Organisms that conduct anaerobic respiration are called *anaerobes*.

Fermentation

Anaerobic respiration doesn't end with glycolysis—only ATP production ends with glycolysis. In anaerobic respiration, *fermentation* takes up where glycolysis leaves off. Let's take a look:

$$1 \text{ glucose} \xrightarrow{\text{glycolysis}} 2 \text{ pyruvic acid}$$

$$2 \text{ pyruvic acid} \xrightarrow{\text{fermentation}} CO_2 \text{ (carbon dioxide) and alcohol (ethanol)}$$

We're looking at what happens to a glucose molecule in a yeast cell or a bacterium. The glucose molecule undergoes fermentation. (This is how we get things like beer and wine.)

Here's another fermentation process: once the cell gets its pyruvic acid, it does this:

$$2 \text{ pyruvic acid} \xrightarrow{\text{fermentation}} \text{lactic acid}$$

(This is how we get things like yogurt.)

When you're doing aerobics, your muscle cells start doing anaerobics. When you exercise to the max, your muscle cells start facing an oxygen shortage. When this happens, even though you are an aerobic organism, your muscle cells start to respire anaerobically. They don't have much choice. Instead of doing:

glycolysis ——> Krebs cycle ——> electron transport chain and oxidative phosphorylation

they do:

glycolysis ——> fermentation

More specifically, they do:

glucose ——> pyruvic acid ——> lactic acid

The lactic acid builds up in your muscles, and before you know it, you've got muscle fatigue.

CHECK YOUR PROGRESS 4

1. All of the following are possible products of fermentation EXCEPT:

    A. lactic acid
    B. carbon dioxide
    C. ethanol
    D. citric acid

2. Which of the following are known to conduct anaerobic respiration?

    I. bacteria
    II. yeast
    III. animal cells

    A. I only
    B. II only
    C. I and II only
    D. I, II, and III

3. Which of the following is NOT an aerobic process?

   A. Fermentation
   B. The Krebs cycle
   C. Oxidative phosphorylation
   D. The electron transport system

4. Glycolysis is a process that does not require oxygen in order to occur. Based on that fact, glycolysis would be considered an _____ process.

5. Muscle fatigue in humans is often due to a build-up of _____ in the [absence ___ presence ____] of oxygen.

6. Which of the following processes yields a net total of 2 ATP?

   I. Glycolysis
   II. Electron transport and oxidative phosphorylation
   III. Fermentation

   A. I only
   B. II only
   C. I and II only
   D. I and III only

7. 1 glucose ——————> pyruvic acid ——————>
   ethanol and _____ _____

8. The sequence shown in question 7 includes which of the following process(es)?

   A. Glycolysis only
   B. Glycolysis and fermentation only
   C. Glycolysis and the Krebs cycle only
   D. Glycolysis, the Krebs cycle, the electron transport chain, and oxidative phosphorylation only

GLOSSARY

acetyl CoA
a 2-carbon molecule produced from pyruvate; joins oxaloacetate to form citrate in the Krebs cycle

aerobes
organisms that conduct aerobic respiration

aerobic respiration
the breakdown of glucose and its successor molecules in the presence of oxygen; relatively efficient yield of ATP

anaerobes
organisms that conduct anaerobic respiration

anaerobic respiration
the breakdown of glucose and its successor molecules in the absence of oxygen; relatively inefficient yield of ATP

citrate
(a.k.a. citric acid) a 6-carbon molecule of the Krebs cycle; formed by the addition of acetyl CoA to oxaloacetate

electron transport chain
an aerobic process in which carrier molecules on the inner mitochondrial membrane transport electrons ultimately to an oxygen molecule

ethanol
an alcohol; an end product of fermentation conducted by yeast and bacteria

FAD
a coenzyme that acts as an electron acceptor; this is its oxidized form

$FADH_2$
a coenzyme that acts as an electron acceptor; this is its reduced form

glycolysis
an anaerobic process in which glucose is broken down into 2 pyruvic acid molecules

Krebs cycle
(a.k.a. the citric acid cycle) an aerobic process; a series of biochemical reactions that take place in the mitochondria

lactic acid
the end product of fermentation in muscle cells and certain fungi and bacteria

matrix
the innermost portion of the mitochondria; it is surrounded by the inner mitochondrial membrane

NAD+

a coenzyme that acts as an electron acceptor; this is its oxidized form

NADH

a coenzyme that acts as an electron acceptor; this is its reduced form

oxaloacetate

a 4-carbon molecule that joins acetyl CoA to create citrate in the Krebs cycle

oxidation

when a molecule gains one or more electrons

oxidative phosphorylation

an aerobic process on the inner mitochondrial membrane that makes use of a proton gradient to produce ATP

pyruvic acid

(a.k.a. pyruvate) the end product of glycolysis

reduction

when a molecule loses one or more electrons

ANSWER KEY

Check Your Progress 1

1. pyruvic acid
2. 2 ATP
3. 2 ATP
4. B

Check Your Progress 2

1. mitochondrion
2. D
3. B
4. B
5. citric acid cycle
6. B

Check Your Progress 3

1. C
2. inner mitochondrial membrane
3. energy
4. proton, ATP
5. A
6. C

Check Your Progress 4

1. D
2. D
3. A
4. anaerobic
5. lactic acid, absence
6. D
7. carbon dioxide (CO_2)
8. B

7

Plant Cells, Tissues, and Activities

PLANT ORGANELLES

Plant cells have all of the organelles that we profiled for animal cells (except centrioles). But what makes plants distinctly plantlike are some special organelles that only they possess. Here's the rundown on distinctive plant organelles.

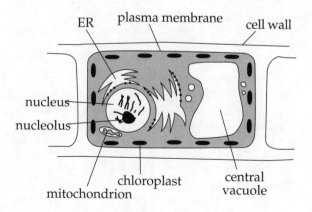

The Cell Wall

This does not replace the cell membrane. It surrounds the cell membrane, so that the first thing you would see if you encountered a plant cell face to face would be a plant cell wall. (Beyond the plant cell wall is the cell membrane.) The plant cell wall is a powerful deterrent to mechanical injury to the cell. Not to mention, its thickness and rigidity protect it from osmotic swelling.

So what's the plant cell wall made of? Mostly cellulose. Recall from chapter 3 that cellulose is a polysaccharide, which means it's a type of carbohydrate.

Chloroplasts

These organelles have a double membrane, like mitochondria do. Inside are more membranes, arranged like stacks of pancakes and connected to one another.

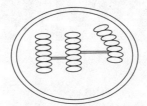

Chloroplasts contain a green pigment called *chlorophyll*. The chlorophyll allows plants to photosynthesize—that is, create sugar molecules out of basic ingredients like water, carbon dioxide, and sunlight. The chlorophyll captures energy from the sun and puts it to work making glucose. Whenever you see this reaction:

$$6CO_2 + 12H_2O \longrightarrow C6H_{12}O_6 + 6H_2O + 6O_2$$

You're looking at the process of photosynthesis written as a chemical reaction. Now you know where this reaction happens—in the chloroplasts of plant cells. Notice that when the plant creates sugar molecules, it also produces some oxygen. Lucky for us, since that's where most of our atmospheric oxygen comes from.

Not All the Producers Live in Hollywood

Here's another thing about photosynthesis: the fact that the plant is able to produce its own food—it doesn't have to eat something in order to get its nutrition—makes it an au-totroph. Another word for autotroph is producer. *(The opposite of an autotroph is a* heterotroph, *or* consumer, *an organism that must get its nutrition by eating something else.)*

Check Your Progress 1

1. Which of the following is NOT true with regard to cellulose?

   A. It is a component of plant cell walls.
   B. It is a polysaccharide.
   C. It protects plant cells from abrasions.
   D. It contains chlorophyll.

2. During the process of photosynthesis, carbon dioxide and water are converted in the presence of sunlight to:

   A. glucose and oxygen.
   B. protein and carbon dioxide.
   C. chlorophyll and protein.
   D. cellulose and glucose.

3. An amateur botanist is looking at 2 plant cells under a microscope. Because he is curious to see what will happen, he removes all of the green pigment from all of the chloroplasts of 1 plant cell. (Don't ask how he accomplished that, but somehow he did.)

   He leaves the other cell alone so that it can be the experimental control. (Controls are extremely important in experimental work, because they give you the normal conditions to compare your results against.) Then he leaves both plant cells in the sun for awhile, to give them a chance to photosynthesize.

   When he later examines both plant cells, he will most likely discover that:

   A. more oxygen is released by the altered cell, because more glucose is being produced.
   B. glucose levels are lower in the altered cell, because carbon dioxide cannot be absorbed.
   C. glucose levels are lower in the altered cell, because energy from sunlight cannot be captured by the chloroplasts.
   D. glucose levels remain the same in both cells, because chlorophyll does not play a role in photosynthesis.

4. If you were preparing to measure relative levels of carbon dioxide and oxygen entering and exiting a plant that is busy photosynthesizing, which of the following hypotheses would you operate under?

   A. Overall, the carbon dioxide would be entering and the oxygen would be leaving the plant cells.
   B. Overall, the oxygen would be entering and the carbon dioxide would be leaving the plant cells.
   C. Overall, both carbon dioxide and oxygen would be leaving the plant cells.
   D. Overall, both carbon dioxide and oxygen would be entering the plant cells.

CROSS-SECTIONAL VIEW OF A LEAF

So you know now that photosynthesis takes place in chloroplasts. Where are all the chloroplasts in a plant? In its leaves. Let's take a closer look. If you were to pick up a leaf and examine a cross-sectional slice of it under a microscope, here's what you'd see:

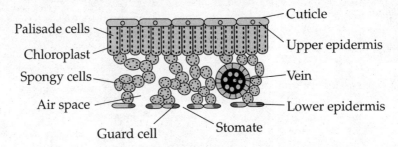

BUSHWACKING THROUGH A LEAF ONE LAYER AT A TIME

There are all sorts of interesting structures in this tissue-paper-thin slice that you'll need to recognize. Let's say for the sake of argument that you were small and dextrous enough to land on a leaf's surface and then tunnel your way through the leaf and out the other side (say you have the afternoon off, and nothing else comes up). Landing on the top of the leaf, you'd have to be careful not to slip on the *cuticle*. The cuticle provides the leaf with a *waxy surface* for protection against moisture loss and nasty mechanical injuries (like the cleats on your boots).

The cuticle is located on the *upper epidermis*, which is the outer cell layer of the leaf (you're standing on it). You can then make your way directly beneath the upper epidermis, to the *palisade cells*. These are easy to spot as tall, column-like cells much like the famous Palisade cliffs on the Hudson River. Rapelling from the top of these cells to the base is quite a job, but you should manage without too much trouble. If you *do* slip on the final descent, luckily you'll land on a *spongy layer*, filled with—what else—*spongy cells*. In between these spongy cells are a lot of air pockets. That knot-like structure to your right is a *leaf vein*, which contains *xylem* and *phloem* tissue.

Now you should have reached the bottom surface of the leaf—the *lower epidermis*. You'll see an opening in the epidermis that you can head for. That opening is called a *stomate*, and the lower epidermis is studded with them. When you reach one you might be stopped short—because it's surrounded on each side by *guard cells*. If you bide your time, at some point the guard cells will move away from the opening, letting you exit through the stomates. You'll be out in time for dinner.

DOING A BACKGROUND CHECK

Now that you're out, you can read up on some of the plant tissues you encountered. The palisade cells contain a lot of chloroplasts, so these are serious photosynthesizing cells. The spongy layer cells also have some chloroplasts. More importantly, however, the air pockets between the loosely packed spongy cells allow for gas exchange. What kinds of gases? Carbon dioxide (CO_2), water (H_2O), and oxygen (O_2). The gases actually get in and out of the leaf through the stomates. (Don't forget that the upper epidermis of the leaf is slicked up with a waxy cuticle, so it's not a good site of gas exchange. Gas exchange can only occur through stomates of the epidermis.)

> Hey, I just waxed that!

On each side of a stomate stands a guard cell. The shape of these guard cells determines whether the stomate will be open, to allow gas exchange, or closed.

A Balancing Act

When there's lots of water around, the guard cells swell up, and in doing so, bulge outward, exposing the stomate. When water's scarce, the guard cells shrink, and they cover the stomate. Why this rather novel form of stomate regulation? Well, if the plant needs water, it doesn't want to lose water through the stomates (water loss by a plant is called transpiration). On the other hand, if the plant has enough water and needs to get its gas exchange going, it can afford to open up its stomates and risk a little water loss.

The leaf vein is made of xylem and phloem. Xylem transports water, and phloem transports food. You know that the food (glucose) comes from photosynthesis; well, the water comes from the roots. *Root hairs* are great absorbers of water and minerals that the rest of the plant depends on for survival. Roots, of course, also keep a plant anchored in the ground; not an insignificant role to a plant.

CHECK YOUR PROGRESS 2

1. Stomates are on _____ the epidermis of a plant leaf that permit the exchange of _____, _____, and _____ between the plant and the environment.

2. What is the function of the guard cells of a plant?

   A. To release a toxic substance when the plant cell is approached by a predator
   B. To provide a seal against mechanical abrasions
   C. To conduct photosynthesis in the presence of sunlight
   D. To regulate the opening and closing of the stomates

3. Chloroplasts are most abundant in a plant's _____ cells.

4. Located directly beneath the plant's cuticle are the

   A. upper epidermal cells
   B. lower epidermal cells
   C. palisade cells
   D. spongy cells

5. A leaf's vein is found among the

   A. palisade cells
   B. epidermal layer
   C. spongy layer
   D. waxy cuticle

6. Within the leaf vein, plant tissue called _____ supplies the leaf with water, and tissue called _____ supplies the leaf with _____.

7. Plant roots absorb _____ and
   _____ and also serve to anchor a
   plant in the soil.

PLANTS WILL BE PLANTS

As amazing as it sounds, plants exhibit certain behaviors. This doesn't mean of course that they can dance on a tabletop when they've had too much water, but it does mean that they show specific responses to certain stimuli. We'll show you what we mean:

- *phototropism*: a plant will grow in the direction of sunlight

- *geotropism*: a plant's roots will always grow downwards towards the center of the earth

- *hydrotropism*: a plant's roots will always grow in the direction of water

- *thigmotropism*: a plant will grow a certain way in response to a solid object (this is how plants grow "along" a windowsill or wooden archway)

The House-bound Plant

IT'S HORMONAL

How do plants manage to behave in these ways? Their hormones allow them to. The hormone called *auxins* make plants grow in general. When amounts of auxin are unevenly distributed in a plant, you get the tropisms we mentioned above. Another popular plant hormone are *gibberellins*. Too many gibberellins make plants grow up tall and spindly.

Name that Tropism

For questions 1 through 3, refer to the following three picture frames below.

1. _____

2. _____

3. _____

Question 4 refers to the illustration below.

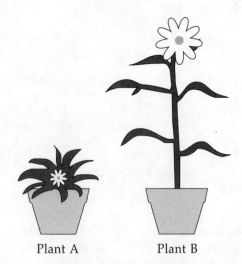

Plant A   Plant B

4. Which one of the two plants above was most likely overdosed with gibberellins? _____

GLOSSARY

autotroph

(a.k.a. producer) an organism that manufactures its own food

auxins

a type of plant hormone; differential amounts make for differential growth rates within a plant

cellulose

a component of plant cell walls; a polysaccharide and carbohydrate

chlorophyll

pigment found within chloroplasts of plants; absorbs energy from sunlight to permit photosynthesis

chloroplast

double-membraned organelle of plant leaf cells (mainly of palisade cells, with some in spongy cells); contain chlorophyll

cuticle

the waxy covering on a leaf's upper epidermis; protects against mechanical abrasions and reduces moisture loss

epidermis

a protective layer of cells found on the outer surfaces of the leaf

experimental control

the "normal" condition of whatever is being tested; used as the standard to measure against results of the experimental manipulation

gibberellins

a type of plant hormone; excess amounts produce plants that are tall and spindly

geotropism

plants will grow in the direction of gravity

guard cells

found at each stomate of a plant leaf; regulate opening and closing of the stomate

heterotroph

(a.k.a. consumer) an organism that must get its source of nutrition by eating other organisms

hydrotropism

plants will grow in the direction of water

leaf vein

contains conducting tissues xylem and phloem to distribute water/dissolved minerals and food, respectively

palisade cells
  tall, columnar layer of cells in a leaf; contain most of a plant's chlorophyll

phloem
  conducting tissue that runs the length of a plant in order to distribute food produced in the leaves to the rest of the plant

photosynthesis
  the production of glucose from the basic materials of carbon dioxide, water, and sunlight

phototropism
  a plant will grow in the direction of sunlight

spongy cells
  loosely packed cells found within the spongy layer of a leaf

spongy layer
  a layer of plant tissue within the leaf; consists of many air pockets and loosely packed cells

transpiration
  water loss by a plant through evaporation

tropism
  the way a plant responds to a stimulus, like sunlight or water or gravity, by growing a certain way

xylem
  conducting tissue which runs from the roots of a plant up the stem and into the leaves to distribute water and dissolved minerals

ANSWER KEY

Check Your Progress 1

1. D
2. A
3. C
4. A

Check Your Progress 2

1. openings; water, carbon dioxide, oxygen
2. D
3. palisade
4. A
5. C
6. xylem; phloem; food
7. water, minerals

Check Your Progress 3

1. phototropism
2. hydrotropism
3. geotropism
4. Plant B

8

DNA, RNA, Transcription, and Translation

CHROMOSOMES

If you take a look at a eukaryote's nucleus, you'll find inside a number of tightly packaged threadlike structures called *chromosomes*. Chromosomes are the cell's way of packing lots of DNA into a very small space (the nucleus). A chromosome is made up mostly of DNA and proteins that are bound into tight formation. We're going to skip about 4 levels of DNA packaging that act to condense it. Instead, we're going to zero in on DNA's most expansive form.

ALL IN THE FAMILY

So what exactly is DNA? For starters, DNA is the stuff of heredity. You got your DNA from your mother and your father. They each got *their* DNA from their mother and father. And so on. DNA gets transmitted directly from parents to offspring. Here's another thing about DNA: it forms the blueprint of who you are. How can it do that? Because it's full of *genes* that code for different *proteins*, and those proteins produce *traits*—like hair color, eye color, double-jointedness, lactose intolerance, female traits and male traits, color blindness, and every other conceivable characteristic that makes up each individual. Amazing!

A CLOSER LOOK

In order to get a better sense of how all of this happens on a molecular level, we need to take a closer look at DNA. We said its full name is *deoxyribonucleic acid*. Now it's time to look at what that is. DNA is made up of lots of smaller repeating units. The units always look like this:

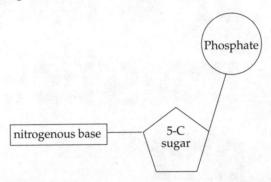

You already know what sugar is from chapter 2. The 5-carbon sugar in DNA is always *deoxyribose*. We can just symbolize phosphate like this:

The sugar and phosphate molecules together are called the DNA's *backbone*, and they never change on a DNA.

Lastly, we have the *nitrogenous bases*. While each DNA subunit always carries the same sugar and the same phosphate, its nitrogenous base varies. There are four possible choices of nitrogenous bases for any given DNA subunit. The choices are:

adenine [A]

guanine [G]

cytosine [C]

thymine [T]

Why are they called nitrogenous bases? Because each contains nitrogen. Luckily for you their molecular structures are not something you have to know.

So each subunit of DNA consists of a 5-carbon sugar, a phosphate, and a nitrogenous base. Another word for this 3-membered subunit is *nucleotide*. DNA is made up of repeating nucleotides whose nitrogenous bases vary.

ONE DNA, COMING UP

Now that we know what subunits we're working with, let's assemble some nucleotides to create a section of DNA. (This will be a very small section—nothing like the 3×10^9 base pairs that you have carefully scrunched up in the nuclei of each one of your cells.)

MAKE IT A DOUBLE

That's one strand of DNA. But eukaryotic DNA is normally *double-stranded*. So we'll create another strand to go along with our original one. But this time we have to pay attention to the bases that are already there, because only certain bases will pair up. [A] will pair with [T] only, and vice versa. [G] will pair with [C] only, and vice versa. Now we're ready to add our second strand. To make things easy, we'll keep the pairing rule in clear view while we work.

FYI

Base-pairing rules:

$$A = T$$
$$C = G$$

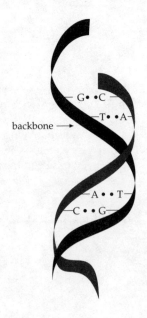

It's a match. Each [T-A] and [G-C] are called a *base pair*. The base pairs are joined together with hydrogen bonds (the very ones you learned about in chapter 1). Hydrogen bonds link each base to its partner.

DO THE TWIST

Now all we have to do is to give our double-stranded molecule a twist. That way our DNA will be arranged in a *double helix*, the normal configuration of eukaryotic DNA.

Characteristics of DNA Data are:

1. It's double-stranded.
2. [A] pairs with [T] and [C] pairs with [G].
3. Its base pairs are joined by hydrogen bonds.
4. It exists as a double helix.

CRACKING THE CODE

We're starting to get somewhere. We're right on the heels of *Watson and Crick*, who trailblazed the double helical structure of DNA. And just like they actually discovered, we're starting to understand that DNA's essence and its power lies in its sequence of nucleotide bases. How so? Because it is the different arrangements of [A], [C], [T], and [G] along the DNA strand that spells out each gene on a DNA molecule. Let's demystify the concept of a gene. We know that each strand of DNA carries a while line-up of basis. Whole sections of those bases make up genes. One gene pretty much calls for the production of one polypeptide. So what is a gene? It's just a series of bases on DNA that together code for a polypeptide. It has a physical beginning and end, and a precise order of bases to it. That's what a gene is.

THINGS HAPPEN—MUTATIONS

Sometimes the precise sequence of bases on a DNA molecule get changed. That's called *mutation*. For instance, part of a gene may specify ATGCTAC and suddenly a mutation arises so that the section now reads: ATACTAC. That switch, from a "G" to an "A" in the third nucleotide, may end up changing the entire character of the protein that the gene had been producing. It may even have the effect of stopping production of the protein entirely. Effects range from not discernible, to inadvertently improving an organism's chance for survival, to devastating and even lethal to the organism. It all depends on the mutation.

So what causes these mutations? Some are spontaneous—they happen on their own, and who knows why. Others are caused by the "big three." From largest to smallest, causes are—chemicals (like components in cigarette smoke, car exhaust, and industry, as well as naturally occurring ones in foods from molds), radiation (including rays from the sun), and viruses.

CHECK YOUR PROGRESS 1

1. Which of the following nucleotide components is a variable?

    A. The phosphate group
    B. The nitrogenous base
    C. The sugar
    D. None of the above

2. Circle the backbone portion of the DNA segment presented below.

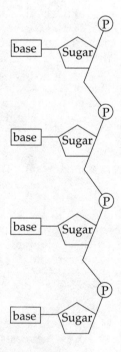

3. Eukaryotic DNA normally exists as a _____-stranded molecule that is shaped in a _____ _____.

4. What kind of bonds join the nitrogenous base pairs of a DNA molecule? _____ _____.

5. Name the four nitrogenous bases that may occur in a DNA's nucleotide subunits.

1. _____
2. _____
3. _____
4. _____

6. According to DNA base-pairing rules,

A. G and T pair up and C and A pair up
B. C and T pair up and A and G pair up
C. C and G pair up and A and T pair up
D. G and A pair up and T and C pair up

REPLICATION—WHEN YOU FEEL LIKE SOME MORE DNA

What if our DNA molecule wants to create more copies of itself? In other words, how does DNA *replicate*? Well, first it needs to create some space in which to work. It will untwist from its helix and separate its strands one section at a time.

Once it has a little elbow room, each separated strand acts as a *template* or blueprint for a new strand to form alongside it. Special enzymes read off the template sequence and respond by bringing nucleotides with bases that follow the base-pairing rules. These nucleotides line up opposite their partners on the template strands.

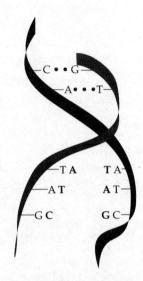

Then bonds form to link up the backbone molecules to one another, and hydrogen bonds form between the template strands' bases and the new strands' bases.

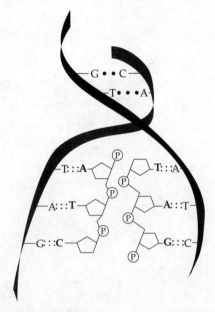

This sequence happens all the way down and up the original DNA molecule. What you have now are two double-stranded DNA molecules when you used to have one double-stranded DNA molecule.

Now let's get this part straight: each new DNA copy strand is *not identical* to its template strand because of our base-pairing rules. Instead each new strand is *complementary* to the template strand—it matches up with the original rather than duplicates the original. Overall, though, the cell now has two identical copies of its original DNA.

SEMICONSERVATIVE REPLICATION—PART OLD, PART NEW

So the way in which a DNA molecule creates more copies of itself is rather unusual. It splits in half lengthwise and then generates a new half to replace each old half. What you get then, are 2 DNAs, each made up of 1 old strand and 1 new strand. This method of replication is called *semiconservative*, because half ("semi") of the original DNA remains (is "conserved") and half is newly made.

CHECK YOUR PROGRESS 2

1. A double-stranded DNA molecule has untwisted and separated in preparation for replication. How many DNA molecules, composed of how many strands, will result?

   A. Four DNA molecules, each composed of two strands
   B. Three DNA molecules, each composed of one strand
   C. Two DNA molecules, each composed of two strands
   D. Two DNA molecules, each composed of one strand

2. During replication of eukaryotic DNA, how many DNA strands act as a template for the synthesis of new DNA?

   A. Four
   B. Two
   C. One
   D. Zero

3. All of the following correctly characterize a newly synthesized DNA strand following replication EXCEPT

    A. its base sequence complements the base sequence of the DNA strand that served as the template.

    B. it has an adenine positioned opposite each thymine on the template strand, and a guanine positioned opposite each cytosine on the template strand.

    C. its backbone structure differs from that of the DNA strand that served as the template.

    D. it constitutes the "new" strand in the double-stranded DNA molecule.

4. *Fill in the numbers that correctly order the replication events listed below.*

    Newly assembled nucleotides are linked up to one another and hydrogen bonds form to join base pairs _____

    Nucleotides line up opposite those on the template strand _____

    Double-stranded DNA untwists and its strands "unzip" _____

5. If you were to examine both strands of double-stranded DNA molecule that was produced via semiconservative replication, what would you find?

    A. Both of its strands were newly synthesized.

    B. One of its strands was newly synthesized, while the other was not.

    C. Neither of its strands was newly synthesized.

    D. None of the above apply.

TRANSCRIPTION AND TRANSLATION—WHEN YOU FEEL LIKE SOME PROTEIN

TRANSCRIPTION

When DNA is interested in making some protein instead, here's what it does. It first has to make some RNA in a process called *transcription*. To start making some RNA, DNA does the same thing it would to make DNA: At one spot it untwists and separates strands some to clear a little space for itself. This time, though, only *part* of the DNA molecule is going to unwind and unzip. The section of DNA that separates contains the gene for the protein the cell wants to make.

FYI

Because this is so important, we'll say it again: All a gene is, is a sequence of nucleotides on the DNA that directs the production of a protein.

gene ——> protein

Each gene codes for a different polypeptide, and polypeptides are the stuff of proteins. Hence the saying, "One gene—one polypeptide." And, it so happens, not all DNA is made up of genes, either. Some segments don't seem to code for anything.

Stop Making Sense

In transcription, only one strand acts as a template, so we'll follow this part very closely. Let's say that our gene has the sequence [T-T-G-C-A-G-A-A] (of course, the real gene sequence would be a lot longer, but you get the idea). We know that the gene's complementary strand has the sequence [A-A-C-G-T-C-T-T]. That complementary strand was an important template when replication was underway. But now that we're into protein production, we're only interested in the gene that directs the production of our one specific protein. For this job, the gene's complementary sequence is considered nonsense, or *antisense*. Because its nucleotide sequence differs from the one on our gene, it would code for an entirely different set of amino acids, therefore an entirely different protein. So it gets ignored. Our gene, called the *sense strand*, gets the action here. Makes sense to us.

Now that we've got that squared, let's look at our gene sequence and see what happens next. As with replication, nucleotides with matching base pairs start lining up opposite the DNA strand. Only these nucleotides are not going to form DNA—they are going to form RNA instead.

About RNA

RNA stands for *ribonucleic* acid. It's a close cousin to DNA. Like DNA, it's a nucleic acid. Also like DNA, it contains nucleotide subunits made of a phosphate group, a 5-carbon sugar, and a nitrogenous base. Both types of nucleic acid have adenine [A], cytosine [C], and guanine [G] as their bases. But here's where RNA is different:

1. It has *ribose* instead of deoxyribose as its sugar.

2. It has *uracil* [U] instead of thymine [T] as one of its bases.

3. It is *single-stranded* instead of double-stranded.

RNA nucleotides line up next to the DNA template. Then, while bonds form to join the RNA nucleotides to one another, this time NO hydrogen bonds will form between the matched DNA-RNA base pairs.

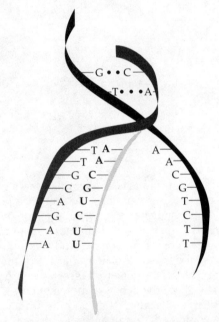

Why not? Because RNA is a single-stranded molecule. Once it's formed, it's heading out of the nucleus and into the cytoplasm. The process we just described—where DNA acts as a template to produce RNA—is called transcription. Because the RNA derived from the DNA template, the RNA in effect bears DNA's message in its structure. For this reason the RNA is called *messenger RNA* (mRNA for short).

CHECK YOUR PROGRESS 3

For questions 1-3, label the following nucleotides as RNA or DNA subunits.

1.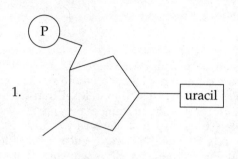

2.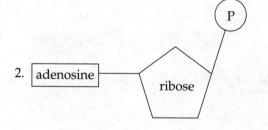

3.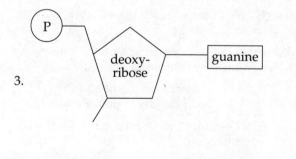

---

4. How many DNA strands act as a template during the process of transcription?

    A. Four
    B. Two
    C. One
    D. Zero

TRANSLATION

In the cytoplasm, the mRNA hooks up with a ribosome (a.k.a. rRNA; remember from chapter 5 that there can be both free and bound ribosomes in a cell) and begins its job of *translation*. In translation, mRNA translates its message from the DNA into production of the protein. Every three bases in an mRNA section codes for a precise amino acid. (That's why a mutation, in which a DNA base sequence gets changed, can have such a big effect. Change the DNA sequence, and you change the mRNA sequence; that may change the amino acid called for, which may change the whole protein, which then changes a trait.) Because each set of three bases on mRNA codes for one amino acid, each threesome is called a *codon*. Let's look over each step by which codons call for specific amino acids to line up.

Steps Involved in Translation

1. mRNA with its sequence of nucleotide bases parks itself at a ribosome in the cytoplasm.

2. individual transfer RNA (tRNA) molecules come along and read the mRNA base sequences three at a time.

3. each tRNA carries its own amino acid (remember that there are 20 different amino acids to choose from).

4. whatever tRNA bonds to the mRNA, hence whatever amino acid it brings over, corresponds to the 3-base sequence the tRNA reads on the mRNA.

5. in this way the mRNA dictates which amino acids will come over, and in which order.

6. once it bonds to the mRNA and drops off its amino acid, each tRNA splits from the scene.

7. each amino acid that gets deposited at the ribosome gets joined to its neighbor amino acids by a peptide bond.

8. the ribosome moves over three more base pairs on the mRNA, to a new sequence.

9. a new tRNA arrives that matches the new sequence, and it brings a new corresponding amino acid.

10. steps 6-8 get repeated.

11. the sequence keeps repeating itself and, before you know it, you have a polypeptide, and then a protein.

Now take a look at the illustration and play out events 1-11 while you're looking. Repeat as often as needed.

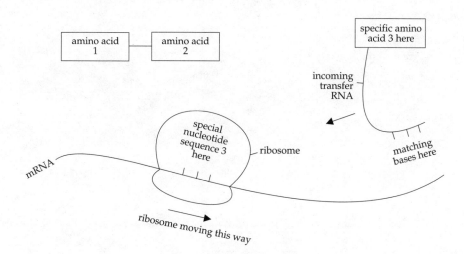

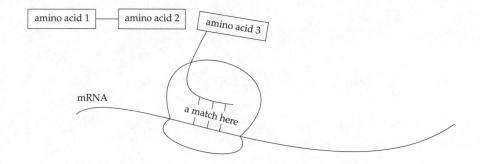

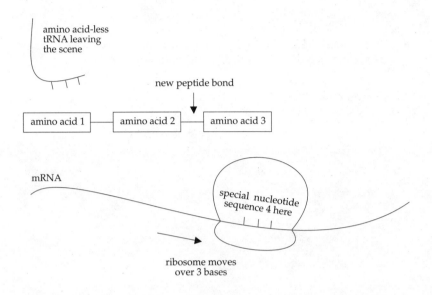

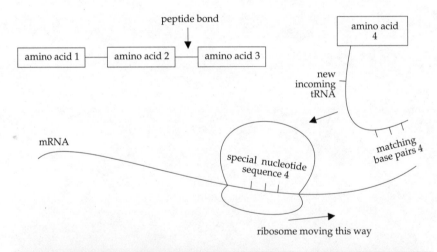

Questions 1-3 refer to the following list. Choose from among the list the best choice that applies to the question.

    A. Replication
    B. Synthesis
    C. Transcription
    D. Translation

1. When DNA makes some RNA

2. When DNA makes some more DNA

3. When RNA makes some protein

4. *Transcriptase* is an enzyme that assists in the process of transcription (not surprisingly). What do you think that *reverse transcriptase*, which is present in certain viruses, does?

    A. Assists in the production of RNA from DNA
    B. Assists in the production of DNA from RNA
    C. Assists in the production of protein from RNA
    D. Assists in the production of RNA from protein

5. Transfer RNA, also known as tRNA, functions in translation in which of the following ways?

    A. It acts as the site of protein synthesis.
    B. It carries a series of nucleotide sequences that dictate the order in which amino acids will be arranged to form a polypeptide.
    C. It supplies the peptide bonds that join individual amino acids into a polypeptide.
    D. It brings a specific amino acid over that corresponds to a sequence of nucleotides on mRNA.

GLOSSARY

adenosine
one of the nitrogenous bases; pairs with thymine in DNA and uracil in RNA

antisense strand
the strand of DNA that does not get translated during transcription

backbone
the molecules that lend stability to the DNA structure; composed of a 5-carbon sugar and phosphate

complement strand
a DNA or RNA strand whose bases match point by point (but do not duplicate) the template strand

cytosine
one of the nitrogenous bases; pairs with guanine in both DNA and RNA

deoxyribose
a 5-carbon sugar found in DNA

DNA
deoxyribonucleic acid; it is heritable; in eukaryotes is double-stranded and a double helix; certain of its sequences of nitrogenous bases constitute genes; its sugar component is deoxyribose

double helix
a slight spiral shape that a double-stranded DNA molecule naturally assumes

gene
a specific sequence of nitrogenous bases that code for the production of a protein

guanine
one of the nitrogenous bases; pairs with cytosine in both DNA and RNA

messenger RNA
a type of RNA which is transcribed from DNA; it carries DNA's instruction for protein synthesis in its nucleotide sequences

mutation
a change in the original base sequence of DNA nucleotides; main causes are spontaneous, chemicals, radiation, and viruses

nitrogenous base
contains nitrogen, component of nucleotides; four possible are cytosine, adenine, thymine, and guanine; uracil instead of thymine in RNA

nucleic acid
DNA and RNA; made up of nucleotide units

nucleotide
subunits of DNA and RNA; made up of a nitrogenous base, a 5-carbon sugar, and a phosphate group

replication
process by which DNA reproduces itself

ribose
a 5-carbon sugar found in RNA

RNA
ribonucleic acid; it is single-stranded and can contain either guanine, adenine, cytosine, or uracil as its bases; its sugar component is ribose

semiconservative replication
DNA reproduction in which each parent strand gives rise to one new strand; the two strands join, thus one-half of the parent molecule is conserved on each round of replication

sense strand
the strand of DNA that acts as template during transcription; it contains the gene of interest

template
the DNA strand whose base sequence guides the construction of a complementary strand alongside it

transcription
process in which RNA is made using a DNA strand as the template

transfer RNA
a type of RNA; each one is able to carry a specific amino acid to the ribosome during protein synthesis

translation
the process of protein synthesis based on mRNA; RNA, and tRNA are also involved

uracil
a nitrogenous base found only in RNA; takes the place of thymine found in DNA

Watson and Crick
these men figured out the double helical structure of the DNA molecule and from that, managed to correctly predict how DNA was able to replicate

ANSWER KEY

Check Your Progress 1

1. B

2.

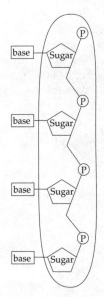

3. double; double helix

4. hydrogen bonds

5. adenine, guanine, cytosine, thymine

6. C

Check Your Progress 2

1. C

2. B

3. C

4. 3, 2, 1

5. B

Check Your Progress 3

1. RNA

2. RNA

3. DNA

4. C

Check Your Progress 4

1. C

2. A

3. D

4. B

5. D

9

Chromosomes, Mitosis, and Meiosis

Where do new cells come from? Old ones. That bit of wisdom is known as the *cell theory* and in biology lingo, one says that new cells arise from pre-existing cells.

In this chapter, we'll take a look how.

PREP WORK

In cell division, one cell divides into two cells. The cell divides up its nuclear material into two (that's called *mitosis*), and it divides up its cyto-plasmic material into two (that's called *cytokinesis*).

Before the cell can begin, though, it has to duplicate its DNA. (If the word "replication" comes to mind, you're right on target. All of the details on replication are there in chapter 8.)

CHROMOSOMES

We humans normally have 46 chromosomes in nearly every one of our cells. We already mentioned that their tight arrangement allows them to squeeze into the small space of the nucleus. Well, here's another thing: our chromo-somes are *paired up*. They come two by two. So, really, we carry *23 pairs* of chromosomes in most of our cells.

These days researchers can do a *karyotype* of anyone's chromosomes: they can isolate the chromosomes, line them up pair by pair, and then study the line-up. All sorts of things can be found by looking at a person's chromosomes that way. Here's what a karyotype of someone's chromosomes looks like:

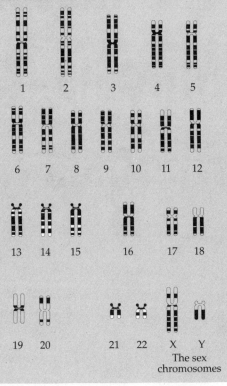

1 2 3 4 5

6 7 8 9 10 11 12

13 14 15 16 17 18

19 20 21 22 X Y
The sex
chromosomes

The line-up comes from *metaphase* chromosomes, which you'll learn all about in a minute.

Ploidy

Because we carry around two copies of DNA in our cells, we are *diploid* (2N) organisms. If we only had one copy of our DNA, we'd be called *haploid* (1N). If we had many copies of our DNA, we'd be called *polyploid*. *Ploidy* refers to the number of copies of DNA that are present in an organism's cells.

Back on Track

Okay, so as we said, we have a cell that is planning to divide. First it must duplicate its DNA. Replication happens, so that 46 individual chromosomes in the cell's nucleus become 92 individual chromosomes. In other words, twenty-three pairs of *single*-stranded chromosomes become 23 pairs of *double*-stranded chromosomes.

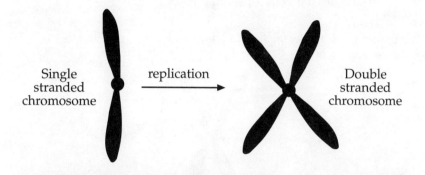

Single stranded chromosome   replication   Double stranded chromosome

FYI

One strand of a double-stranded chromosome is called a *chromatid*. If you look at just one double-stranded chromosome, each of its strands is called a *sister chromatid*. The *centromere* is the part of a double-stranded chromosome where the two chromatids attach.

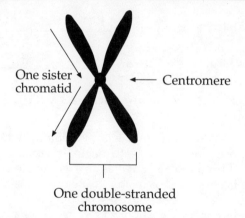

One sister chromatid   ←— Centromere

One double-stranded chromosome

Our cell replicated its DNA during *interphase*, the nondividing phase of its cycle. (During interphase, the chromosomes are nice and loose; you can't even make them out under a microscope if you looked.) Next the cell heads into *mitosis*, the dividing phase of its cycle.

CHECK YOUR PROGRESS 1

1. How many copies of chromosomes are normally found in the cells of a diploid organism?_____

Questions 2-5 refer to the illustration of a human chromosome shown below.

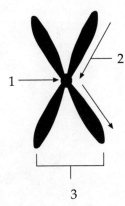

2. What is structure 1 called? _____

3. What is structure 2 called? _____

4. What is structure 3 called? _____

5. What can you say about structure 3 with reasonable certainty?

    A. It is from a cell that has just completed mitosis and is ready to begin interphase.

    B. It is from a cell that has just completed replication and is ready to begin mitosis.

    C. It is from a cell that has not recently undergone replication and is not prepared to begin mitosis.

    D. It is from a cell that has just completed interphase and is ready to begin replication.

MITOSIS—PMAT

In mitosis, the nuclear material—the chromosomes, which contain the DNA—divide in two.

The four stages of mitosis are: *prophase, metaphase, anaphase,* and *telophase*—PMAT for short.

Prophase

The first stage of mitosis is prophase. What happens during prophase is just about what you would expect to happen at the onset of cell division, if you thought about it.

1. The chromosomes *condense* (draw tighter together). Now you can see them under a microscope if you looked. (Condensing the chromosomes makes them easier to deal with, and provides less likelihood for mistakes when they get divided up. Think about it this way: would you rather parcel out some tightly coiled spools of thread, or some loose, unraveled ones? One of these choices leads to a real tangle.)

2. The nuclear membrane begins to dissolve. (How else can the chromosomes inside the nucleus get separated out to two different cells?)

3. The mitotic spindle forms. (This is a type of cell scaffolding made out of microtubules. It will help to align the chromosomes as they move to separate cells.) At each end or pole of the cell, the centrioles anchor the mitotic spindle.

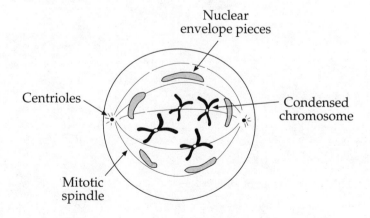

Nuclear envelope pieces

Centrioles

Condensed chromosome

Mitotic spindle

Metaphase

The second stage of mitosis is metaphase. Here's where each chromosome lines up at the metaphase plate at the equator of the cell. They get help in lining up from the *mitotic spindle*.

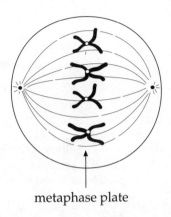

metaphase plate

Anaphase

In the third phase of mitosis—anaphase—the centromeres split, the sister chromatids separate, and each one moves to opposite poles of the cell. Again, the mitotic spindle helps to bring this about.

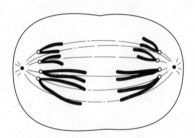

Telophase

Now that the two sets of chromatids are at opposite poles of the cell, the last phase of mitosis—telophase—begins. The events of telophase are about what you'd expect after the nuclear material has been divided in two. The cell is ready to get back to its normal state. So it pretty much does the reverse of what it did during prophase:

1. The chromosomes decondense.

2. The nuclear envelope starts to form around each set of chromosomes.

3. The mitotic spindle begins to dissemble.

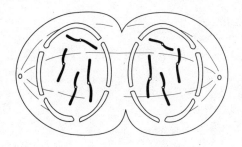

MITOSIS IS OVER, BUT OUR CELL'S NOT DONE YET

Now that the nuclear stuff has divided into two, it's time for the cell body—the cytoplasm and everything it contains—to split. This event begins about the same time that telophase is going on. It's called cytokinesis. Right about in the middle of the two separate groups of chromosomes, the cell body divides in two.

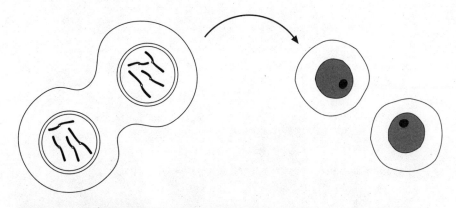

FYI

If it's an animal cell, the cell membrane *pinches in* (furrows) on each side. It continues to pinch in until two new cells are formed.

If it's a plant cell, a *cell plate* originates at the center of the cell and grows outwards, separating the plant cell in two.

YOU GET WHAT YOU STARTED WITH— ONLY DOUBLE THE NUMBER

Once mitosis and then cytokinesis are finished, what was once a single diploid (2N) cell has now become two daughter diploid (2N) cells. Where there was one cell, there are now two, and they each contain the exact same nuclear material.

CHECK YOUR PROGRESS 2

Questions 1-5 refer to the answer choices listed below.

   A. Interphase
   B. Mitosis
   C. Replication
   D. Cytokinesis

1. Occurs during interphase _____

2. The process by which the cell cytoplasm and its contents are divided into two _____

3. The act by which single-stranded chromosomes become double-stranded _____

4. Nondividing stage of a cell cycle_____

5. Encompasses the stages prophase, metaphase, anaphase, and telophase _____

6. What is the name of the structure that joins two sister chromatids together? _____

7. List 3 cellular events that take place during prophase of mitosis.

   1. _____

   2. _____

   3. _____

8. All of the following take place during telophase of mitosis EXCEPT

   A. chromosomes decondense
   B. the nuclear membrane reforms
   C. the mitotic spindle disassembles
   D. sister chromatids move to opposite poles of the cell

9. During metaphase of mitosis:

   A. the nuclear envelope disintegrates
   B. sister chromatids line up at the equator of the cell
   C. sister chromatids decondense
   D. sister chromatids move to opposite poles of the cell

10. What happens during anaphase of mitosis?

   _____

11. During cytokinesis in the plant cell, a _____ _____ originates at the center of the cell and spreads outwards, dividing the plant cell body in two.

12. At the end of mitosis

   A. one (2N) cell has given rise to two (2N) cells
   B. one (2N) cell has given rise to two (1N) cells
   C. one (1N) cell has given rise to two (2N) cells
   D. one (1N) cell has given rise to two (1N) cells

SEXUAL VS. ASEXUAL REPRODUCTION

The type of cell division that we just looked at—mitosis—is a form of *asexual reproduction*. Each new daughter cell is exactly like the parent cell; its chromosomes are an exact duplicate of the original cell's. Now we are going to look at a process that makes *sexual reproduction* possible. In sexual reproduction, haploid nuclei from two different sources fuse to create a diploid organism. The diploid organism has a new and different set of DNA than either of its parents has.

Could mitosis produce the kind of cells that are capable of fusing during sexual reproduction? No way—because they are *already* diploid. If two diploid cells were to fuse, you'd get a polyploid cell, which would self-destruct. Since sexual reproduction hasn't yet come to a screeching halt, where are all the haploid cells coming from?

MEIOSIS

Meiosis is the process in which diploid cells undergo cell division to produce haploid cells. Since in meiosis one starts with a 2N cell and ends up with 1N cells, this kind of cell division is called *reduction division*. The nuclear material gets reduced by half. Haploid (1N) cells are just what's needed to fuel sexual reproduction. In males, the haploid "sex cell" that fuels sexual reproduction is the sperm cell. In females, it is the ovum, or egg cell (we'll have more to say about this in chapter 12).

Do Not Pass Go

We'll tell you right now that before the diploid cell undergoes meiosis, it replicates, just as it would for mitosis. So here's a conundrum: the cell makes *double* its normal amount of nuclear material even though it has to divest itself of *half* of it. What solution is there to this predicament? To undergo *two* divisions instead of one, without stopping in between to make more DNA.

Round One

The first round of cell division in meiosis has stages pretty much just like the ones in mitosis—there's *prophase I, metaphase I, anaphase I,* and *telophase I.* (Here we put a I after each stage, to distinguish from the second round of division.) However, there are a few MAJOR DIFFERENCES in the first round of meiosis.

1. During metaphase I of meiosis, double-stranded chromosomes line up in *pairs*. (In mitosis chromosomes lined up *singly*—independently of each other. Flip back to Figure 9.6 to compare.) Each pair of chromosomes is called a *homologous pair*. They're not precisely alike—that's why they're not called an identical pair—but they're very closely matched to one another in terms of the genes that they carry. (How many homologous pairs of chromosomes exist in humans? 23.)

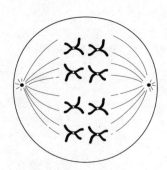

Meet Me at the Metaphase Plate

Sear prophase I of meiosis into your brain for this reason:
It's when synapsis occurs. Chromosome pairs line up so that
the homologues are side by side. Their close proximity to
each other is known as synapsis.

During synapsis, homologous chromosomes can take advantage of their nearness to one another to undergo
crossing over. In crossing over, one or more sections of
chromatid from one chromosome can exchange with corresponding sections of chromatid from its homologous
chromosome.

This careful mix-and-matching creates even more genetic
variation in meiosis. The resulting DNA content ends up
even more different from the original DNA content. This
happens to be the crux of sexual reproduction—to introduce genetic variation.

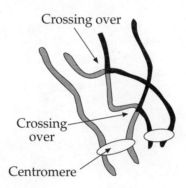

2. During anaphase I of meiosis, double-stranded chromosomes remain intact as they move to opposite poles of
   the cell. Sister chromatids don't separate. (In mitosis they
   do; flip back to Figure 9.7 to compare.)

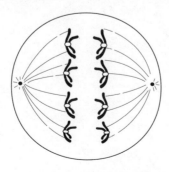

3. By telophase, each set of chromosomes at the opposite poles of the cell are haploid: they don't have an extra copy of chromosomes anymore. But they do have a duplicate, unlike in mitosis. (Check out Figure 9.8 to see the difference for yourself.)

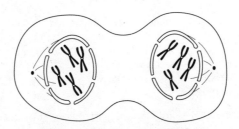

So our meiosis chromosomes at telophase I are still double-stranded. Not for long, though. After cytokinesis, the two haploid daughter cells are ready for round two.

ROUND TWO

Now comes the easy part—*prophase II*, *metaphase II*, *anaphase II*, and *telophase II* of meiosis are really just like the stages of mitosis. We're down to single chromosomes that are double-stranded, and they line up one by one at the metaphase plate; the centromeres split, and each sister chromatid moves to an opposite pole. Cytokinesis finishes up the cell division.

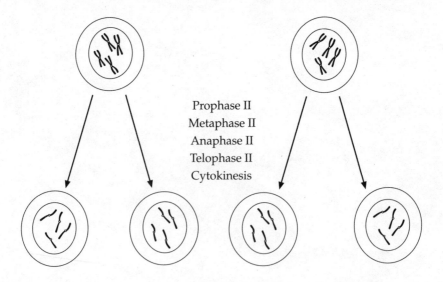

Prophase II
Metaphase II
Anaphase II
Telophase II
Cytokinesis

In meiosis, you started with one cell and you end up with four.

You started with a diploid (2N) cell and you end up with haploid (1N) ones.

The nuclear contents of your daughter cells don't match each other, nor do they match the nuclear contents of the parent cell: some genetic variation's been introduced.

Because learning the particulars of mitosis and meiosis irritates so many students, we're going to give you a break here and grill you in the form of a crossword puzzle. Grab something refreshing to drink, stretch out, and rev up those brain cells.

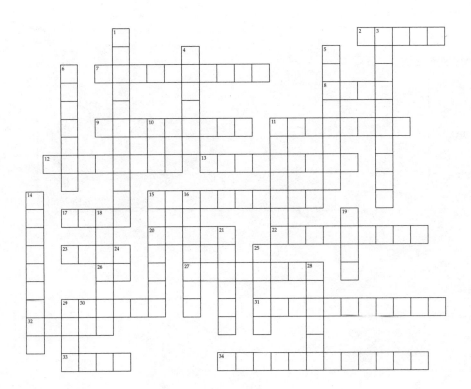

Across

2   What an animal cell membrane does during cytokinesis

7   Holds sister chromatids together

8   Number of diploid cells left following telophase I of meiosis

9   What divides during cytokinesis

11   The mitotic spindle —— during prophase

12   Name given to cells following mitosis

13   Stage of chromosomal alignment

15   Similar, not identical

17   What nuclei do during sexual reproduction

20 Way in which chromosomes travel during metaphase I of meiosis

22 What a nuclear envelope does prior to metaphase

23 What a homologous chromosome is not

26 Whether or not mitosis produces genetic variation

27 Opportunity for crossing over

29 Ploidy number during meiosis is ——-

31 Happens during interphase

32 Required for cytokinesis in plants is the cell ——-

33 Product number in meiosis

34 What a mitotic spindle does at telophase

Down

1 Number of paired chromosomes in a human

3 Nondividing stage of the cell cycle

4 Metaphase chromosomes are —— -stranded

5 What chromosomes do during prophase

6 Reproduction that does not involve a change in number or content of original DNA

10 Copies of DNA in a haploid cell

11 Humans' ploidy status

14 DNA line-up

15 Product of meiosis

16 Reduction division

18 Mitotic ——-

19 What nuclear membranes do at telophase

21 Chromosome strands at telophase II

24 Whether or not cells during mitosis undergo synapsis

25 Haploid cells of males

28 What a centromere does during anaphase

29 Chromosome content at start of prophase II, vs. original content

30 Homologous chromosomes line up —— the metaphase plate

GLOSSARY

anaphase
> stage of cell division involving separation of chromosomes to opposite poles of a cell

asexual reproduction
> involves only one parent; no change in chromosome content or number as a result

cell plate
> acts to separate daughter cells during cytokinesis in plant cells

cell theory
> the premise that new cells arise from pre-existing ones (as opposed to out of thin air)

chromatid
> a single strand of a double-stranded chromosome

chromosome
> a tightly arranged structure composed mainly of DNA and protein; found in nucleus

crossing over
> occurs during metaphase I of meiosis; chromatid segments exchange at corresponding points; produces genetic variation

cytokinesis
> division of cell cytoplasm; involves a pinching in of the animal cell membrane and development of a cell plate in plant cells

diploid
> two copies of chromosomes

genetic variation
> even within a particular species (which share many genes in common) there are differences among each individual's genome, or genetic make-up.

haploid
> one copy of chromosomes

interphase
> nondividing stage of a cell cycle

homologous chromosomes
> a pair of chromosomes in a diploid cell; they match each other very closely, but they are not identical

karyotype
> a line-up of metaphase chromosomes that reveals all sorts of things by the sizes, shapes, banding patterns, and number of chromosomes present

metaphase
> stage of cell division during which chromosomes line up at the metaphase plate at the equator of the cell

meiosis
> also called reduction division; a nuclear division in which the chromosome amount is halved; consists of two successive divisions

mitosis
> stage of a cell cycle during which the nuclear material divides; consists of prophase, metaphase, anaphase, and telophase

mitotic spindle
> microtubule structure assembled during prophase of mitosis; assists in orienting and moving chromosomes during cell division

ploidy
> copy number of chromosomes

polyploid
> many copies (>2) of chromosomes

prophase
> stage of cell division characterized by condensing chromosomes, dissolution of the nuclear membrane, and development of the mitotic spindle

sexual reproduction
> involves two different parents; entails fusion of both parents' nuclei; results in a change in chromosomal content

sister chromatid
> one of two strands in a double-stranded chromosome

synapsis
> a close positioning of homologous chromosomes during prophase I that provides an opportunity for crossing over to occur

telophase
> an end-stage of cell division during which the nuclear envelope re-establishes itself, the mitotic spindle dissembles, and the chromosomes decondense

ANSWER KEY

Check Your Progress 1

1. 2N

2. centromere

3. chromatid

4. double-stranded chromosome

5. B

Check Your Progress 2

1. C

2. D

3. C

4. A

5. B

6. centromere

7. chromosomes condense; nuclear envelope dissolves; mitotic spindle forms

8. D

9. B

10. sister chromatids move to opposite poles of the cell

11. cell plate

12. A

Check Your Progress 3

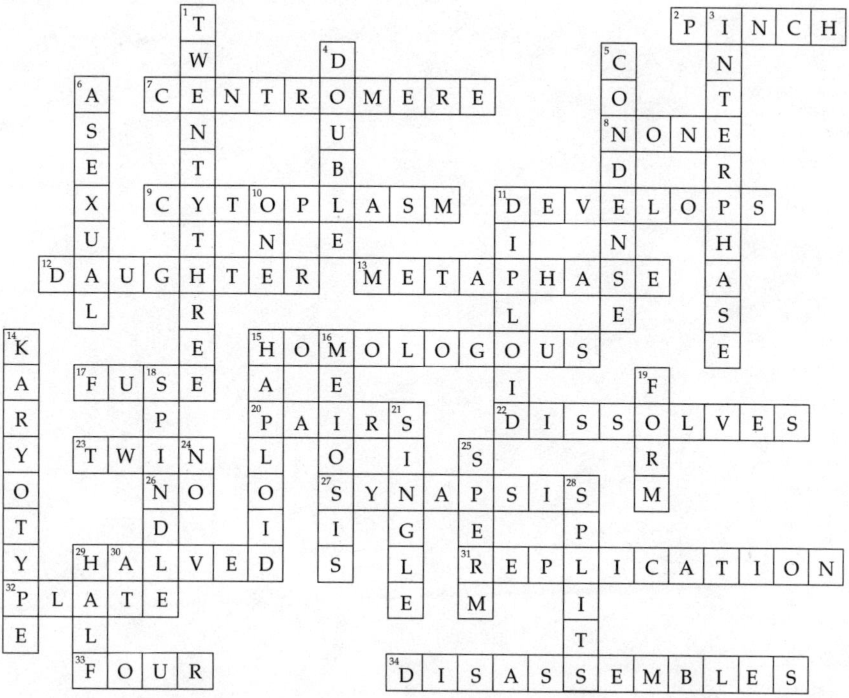

CHAPTER 10

Gametogenesis, Fertilization, and Development

GAMETES: NOT YOUR NORMAL CELLS

While nearly all of your cells are diploid, those of your cells that can partici-
pate in sexual reproduction are haploid, and they're produced by meiosis.
These special cells are called *gametes*, or sex cells. *Gametogenesis* is the name
given to the formation of the gametes. Where does gametogenesis happen?
In the *gonads*.

It's a Girl Thing

The female's gonads are her *ovaries*. It is there that she produces ova (*ovum*
for one), or egg cells, which are the female gamete. *Oogenesis* is the specific
name for producing ova. And here's a funny thing about oogenesis: Even
though four cells get produced during meiosis, three of the cells eventually
drop out as *polar bodies*, so only one ovum remains.

It's a Boy Thing

The male's gonads are his *testes*. That's where he produces *sperm* cells, the
male gamete. *Spermatogenesis* is the specific name for producing sperm.
Meiosis yields four haploid cells, and all four mature and are modified to
become sperm cells.

FERTILIZATION

Fish do it, frogs do it, humans do it—engage in fertilization, that is. It's how they perpetuate their species. In the case of fish and frogs, fertilization is *external*—it takes place outside of the body. In humans, fertilization is an *internal* event. The male's sperm cells use their flagella to swim up through the female's vagina, past the uterus, and up to the fallopian tubes, where fertilization actually happens.

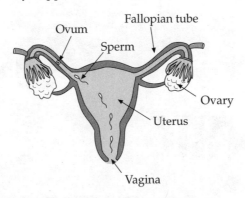

A Chance Encounter

In one of the fallopian tubes—if the timing is right—a female's ovum, or egg, has been released by an ovary and is on its way down towards the uterus. When one or more sperm cells intercept the ovum, the first one to actually penetrate the ovum's outer layers and fuse its nucleus with the ovum's nucleus *fertilizes* the ovum. At this point we don't have a sperm and an ovum anymore; we have a *zygote* on our hands. A zygote is a fertilized egg.

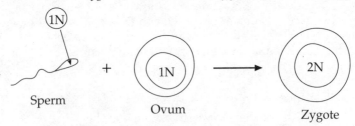

We All Know That 1 + 1 = 2

An ovum is a haploid cell, and so is a sperm cell. When the ovum's (1N) nucleus fuses with the sperm's (1N) nucleus, you get a zygote with a diploid nucleus (2N). Each gamete contributed one copy of DNA to the zygote. That's good, because humans are diploid creatures. They need to carry around 2 copies of their DNA in each of their cells, except for their sex cells.

---

1. Is a gamete haploid or diploid?

   _____

2. Is a zygote haploid or diploid?

   _____

3. How many sperm cells are produced by spermatogenesis?

   _____

4. How many ova are produced by oogenesis?

   _____

5. Where does gametogenesis take place in the female?

   _____

6. What is the name of the male gonad?

   _____

EMBRYONIC DEVELOPMENT

Now let's think about this for a minute. For any species, how is one tiny fertilized egg going to end up as a complete little organism at birth? For one thing, it had better start dividing. For another, it had better start shifting around and organizing those new cells. So that's what it does.

Hitting the Ground Running

As soon as a zygote is created, it starts to divide—over and over again. This series of mitotic divisions is called *cleavage*. One cell becomes two, two becomes four, four becomes eight, eight becomes sixteen, and, fast and furious, a few hundred cells get created. During this time, the embryo itself doesn't get a whole lot bigger, but the number of cells it contains sure does.

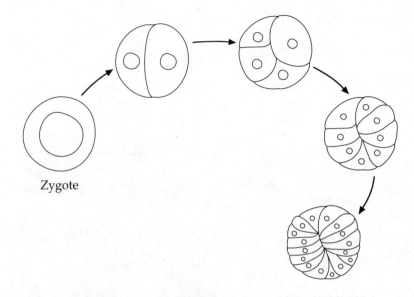

Zygote

In the next stage of development, all those new cells arrange into a fluid-filled ball called the *blastula*.

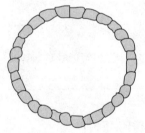

Blastula (cross-section)

Next the blastula indents at one section and, in doing so, creates the *gastrula*. This stage of development is called *gastrulation*. An important event happens during gastrulation. As the cells of the embryo migrate to different areas, they become different from each other. As a result, three distinct *germ cell layers* form. The innermost layer is called the *endoderm*; the middle layer the *mesoderm*; and the outer layer the *ectoderm*. The germ cell layers will give rise to all of the organs of the body.

Who Becomes What

1. Ectoderm—the outer layer—becomes skin (epidermis), nervous system and eyes

2. Endoderm—the inner layer—becomes the linings of the digestive tract and its offshoots, including the respiratory system

3. Mesoderm—the middle layer—becomes most of everything else, like skeleton, muscles, the reproductive, circulatory, and excretory systems, to name a few

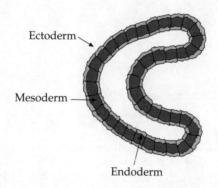

Gastrula (cross-section)

After gastrulation in a vertebrate embryo comes *neurulation*. In neurulation, the *neural tube* forms. The neural tube will eventually develop into the brain and the spinal cord.

Rewind

Let's do a quick recap of the early stages of embryonic development. A zygote undergoes cleavage and then becomes in quick succession a blastula, then a gastrula, then a neurula.

Fast Forward

Once the early stages are completed the embryo's cells continue to differentiate, its organs and systems develop, and the embryo grows larger, until it becomes a fully formed little organism. These later stages make for entire books in themselves, but for us, they are stories for another day.

CHECK YOUR PROGRESS 2

Questions 1-4 refer to the answer choices listed below.

A. Neurula
B. Blastula
C. Zygote
D. Gastrula

1. Fluid-filled ball of cells ________________

2. Contains the three germ cell layers: ectoderm, mesoderm, and endoderm ________________

3. Fertilized egg ________________

4. Contains the precursor structure to the brain and spinal cord ________________

5. At the blastula stage a human embryo implants into the lining of the uterus. In which of the following structures did fertilization take place?

   A. The vagina
   B. The uterus
   C. The fallopian tubes
   D. The ovaries

6. During cleavage

   A. the embryo grows larger in size
   B. a series of meiotic divisions ensues
   C. 2N cells produce 1N cells
   D. 2N cells produce more 2N cells

7. Which of the following structures derives from ectoderm?

   A. The blood vessels
   B. The eye
   C. The inner lining of the digestive tract
   D. The muscles

8. Which of the following correctly orders the early stages of embryonic development?

A. Zygote → fertilization → cleavage → gastrula → neurula → blastula

B. Gastrula → blastula → neurula → cleavage → fertilization → zygote

C. Fertilization → blastula → gastrula → neurula → cleavage → zygote

D. Fertilization → zygote → cleavage → blastula → gastrula → neurula

GLOSSARY

blastula
: a fluid-filled ball of cells; present during early embryonic development

blastulation
: the process by which a fluid-filled ball of cells is created during embryonic development

cleavage
: a series of rapid mitotic divisions of the zygote

differentiation
: the process by which cells become different from one another

ectoderm
: the outer layer of the germ cell layers; goes on to produce the epidermis, nervous system, and the eyes

endoderm
: the inner layer of the three germ cell layers; goes on to produce the inner linings of the digestive tract and its offshoots, including the respiratory tract

fallopian tubes
: the right and left fallopian tubes of the female are passageways through which the ovum travels from the ovary to the uterus; they also are the site of fertilization

fertilization
: the process by which the ovum is penetrated by the sperm cell and sperm and ovum nuclei fuse to form a diploid zygote

gametes
: (a.k.a. sex cells); haploid cells; the product of meiosis; in females it is the ova (eggs) and in males it is the sperm

gametogenesis
: the act by which the gametes are produced; requires meiosis

gastrula
: an early embryonic structure composed of three distinct layers of cells: the ectoderm, mesoderm, and endoderm

gastrulation
: the process by which the gastrula forms; the blastula invaginates (indents) at one face and migrating cells produce the three germ layers of the gastrula

germ cell layers
: the ectoderm, mesoderm, and endoderm of the gastrula; these give rise to all of the structures of the organism

gonads

produce the gametes; in males the testes; in females, the ovaries

mesoderm

the middle layer of the three germ layers; gives rise to such structures as connective tissue, blood vessels and cells, the skeleton, and muscle cells

neural tube

the precursor structure to the brain and spinal cord of vertebrates

neurulation

the process by which the neural tube develops in a vertebrate embryo

oogenesis

the process by which the female gametes—ova—are produced in the ovaries

ovaries

the female gonads; oogenesis occurs here

ovum

(a.k.a. egg); the female gamete; haploid product of meiosis; fuses with sperm to produce a zygote

polar bodies

those products of meiosis during oogenesis that disintegrate

sperm

the male gamete; haploid product of meiosis; fuses with ovum to produce a zygote

spermatogenesis

the process by which the male gametes—the sperm—are produced in the testes

testes

the male gonads; spermatogenesis occurs here

zygote

a fertilized ovum; it is diploid as a result of fusion of male and female haploid nuclei

ANSWER KEY

Check Your Progress 1

1. haploid
2. diploid
3. four
4. one
5. the ovaries
6. the testes

Check Your Progress 2

1. B
2. D
3. C
4. A
5. C
6. D
7. B
8. D

11

Human Physiology I

THE RESPIRATORY SYSTEM, CIRCULATORY SYSTEM, EXCRETORY SYSTEM, AND DIGESTIVE SYSTEM

THE RESPIRATORY SYSTEM

What makes up the air that we breathe? Mostly nitrogen (78%), some oxygen (20%), a little bit of carbon dioxide, and even less of some other stuff, like helium. Our respiratory system is interested in the oxygen. With the help of the rib cage, a muscle called the *diaphragm* acts to pull air into our lungs (that's called *inspiration*). Then the oxygen moves from our lungs and into all of our tissues, where we need it. Meanwhile, we get rid of carbon dioxide, which has built up in our tissues, by breathing it out of our lungs. Let's take a closer look.

THINGS KEEP GETTING SMALLER

When you breathe in, air enters your mouth and nose, and passes through your *trachea* (a.k.a. *windpipe*). Your trachea is ringed with *cartilage* to help keep it open. Now here's where things get interesting: from your trachea all the way down to the very end of your airway, the air enters a maze created by no fewer than 23 sets of branching.

Branching produces a lot of surface area, which is just what an organ that conducts gas exchange needs.

How are those 23 sets of branching accomplished? Like this. At the end of your trachea are your *bronchi*, which branch left and right. Just past each bronchus, your respiratory tract branches into a bunch of *bronchioles*. Each bronchiole branches out into many smaller offshoots. At the end of each offshoot is a small sac called an *alveolus* (the plural is *alveoli*).

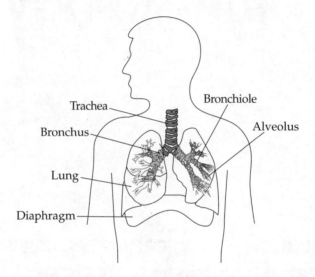

The *lungs* (you've got two of them) are the organs that carry out the gas exchange. They include the bronchi, bronchioles, and the alveoli.

Oxygen can pass right through alveoli, because gases can undergo diffusion. The alveoli are made up of one thin, moist layer of cells, an ideal arrangement for diffusion. Where is this oxygen headed? To capillaries positioned right on the other side of the alveoli. Also one-cell thin, the capillaries are very tiny blood vessels that offer an easy target for diffusion.

A Trade Agreement Amongst Your Cells

Inside the lung capillaries is blood that contains lots of carbon dioxide and very little oxygen. That's a perfect match, because inside the alveoli is air that contains lots of oxygen and very little carbon dioxide. So a trade-off ensues: carbon dioxide leaves the capillaries and enters the alveoli (all by diffusion), and oxygen leaves the alveoli and enters the capillaries (also all by diffusion).

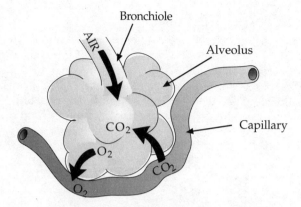

Of course this exchange makes perfect sense, because most of us know that we need oxygen and that we breathe out carbon dioxide.

HEMOGLOBIN'S ROLE

So oxygen diffuses from the alveoli and enters our blood stream, to be carried to all of our tissues. In the blood stream, the oxygen molecules attach to a protein in red blood cells called *hemoglobin*.

When You're Tired All the Time

Since hitching a ride with hemoglobin is the only way that oxygen travels in your blood stream, you run into trouble if you don't have enough hemoglobin, which happens in a condition called anemia.

ANOTHER EXCHANGE AT THE TISSUES

When the blood with its oxygen-carrying hemoglobin enter capillaries in the tissues, the oxygen hops off the hemoglobin molecules and diffuses into the tissues, where it will be used (we hope you remember from Chapter 5) during aerobic cellular respiration. At the same time, carbon dioxide produced in the tissues diffuses into the blood stream, to be carried to the lungs.

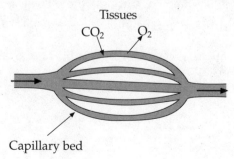

The Carbon Dioxide Gets Exhaled

We said that at the lungs, carbon dioxide diffuses out of the blood stream and into the alveoli. In short order it is breathed out of the airways (that's called *expiration*). Carbon dioxide follows the same route that air followed—but in reverse. It first passes through the bronchioles, then the bronchus, the trachea, and finally the mouth or nose—perhaps borne along by a big dramatic sigh, an exclamation, or simply a quiet and unassuming breath out.

Check Your Progress 1

1. If you were a molecule of inspired oxygen, what route would you take through the airways?

   A. Bronchioles, bronchus, trachea, alveoli, mouth or nose
   B. Mouth or nose, bronchus, bronchioles, alveoli, trachea
   C. Mouth or nose, trachea, bronchus, bronchioles, alveoli
   D. Alveoli, bronchioles, bronchus, trachea, mouth or nose

2. If you were a molecule of carbon dioxide, what route would you take through the airways?

   A. Bronchioles, bronchus, trachea, alveoli, mouth or nose
   B. Mouth or nose, bronchus, bronchioles, alveoli, trachea
   C. Mouth or nose, trachea, bronchus, bronchioles, alveoli
   D. Alveoli, bronchioles, bronchus, trachea, mouth or nose

3. What is the name of the muscle that, together with the rib cage, produces the act of inspiration?

   _____

4. During inspiration

   A. air is pulled into the lungs
   B. oxygen is transferred from the lungs to the capillaries
   C. air is released from the lungs to the outside of the body
   D. carbon dioxide is released from the lungs to the outside of the body

5. All of the following are true concerning hemoglobin EXCEPT

   A. it is a protein
   B. it is found in white blood cells
   C. it transports oxygen from the lungs to the rest of the body tissues
   D. its amounts are deficient in anemia

6. In what directions do oxygen and carbon dioxide molecules diffuse across the capillaries in the body tissues?

   oxygen molecules: _____

   carbon molecules:_____

7. What ultimately happens to the carbon dioxide that is produced in the body tissues?

   _____

THE CIRCULATORY SYSTEM

We mentioned how the blood stream carries oxygen and carbon dioxide to their different destinations. Well, the blood stream wouldn't be headed anywhere if it weren't for the pumping action of a muscular organ called the heart. The four chambers of the heart are the *left* and *right atria*, and the *left* and *right ventricles*.

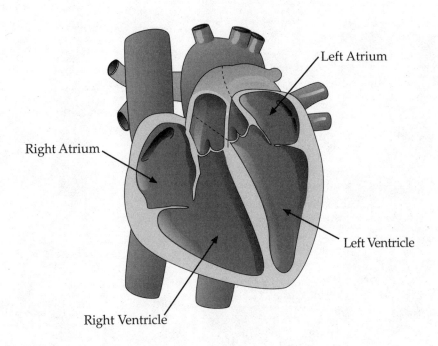

Left Atrium

Right Atrium

Left Ventricle

Right Ventricle

An Open and Shut Case

In some organisms, the circulatory system is an open one, meaning that the blood gets pumped from the heart into a general body cavity and directly sloshes up against the cells. The grasshopper has this type of circulation. Other organisms, such as earthworms, frogs, and mammals like us, have a closed circulatory system: blood is pumped from the heart into a series of blood vessels of different sizes, and the blood never makes direct contact with the cells themselves. It's more efficient that way.

In humans, blood flows in a continuous circuit. Just as it would be impossible to say at which point a circle actually begins and ends, it is impossible to say where blood flow begins and ends. We can pick an arbitrary starting point, however, in order to make sense of the process. We'll start at the left atrium of the heart.

Blood enters the left atrium through the *pulmonary veins*. The blood just came from the lungs, so it has a lot of oxygen in it, and not much carbon dioxide. The left atrium contracts, pushing this blood through a valve and into the left ventricle. Now the left ventricle contracts and forces the blood out through the *aorta*.

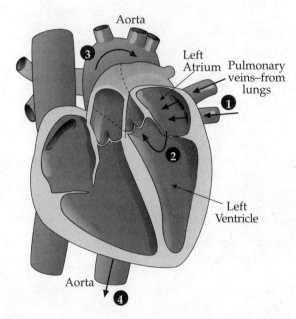

1 blood from lungs enters left atrium through pulmonary veins

2 blood from left atrium moves to left ventricle

3 from left ventricle blood moves into aorta

4 blood leaves aorta

Know Your Blood Vessels

The aorta is an *artery*, and arteries always carry blood away from the heart. Arteries branch into smaller *arteries*, which eventually branch into even narrower *arterioles*. The arterioles lead directly into *capillaries*.

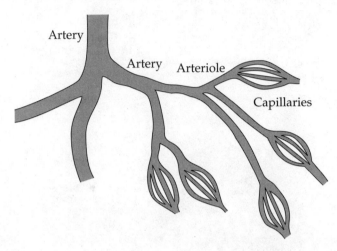

By the time we're talking capillaries, we're deep into the body tissues. The one-cell-thick capillaries ensure that all parts of the body—however far from the heart—get access to the blood and its contents.

What's Really in the Red Stuff

We all can recognize blood on sight—it's that distinctive. That's why movie-makers go to great lengths to create a reasonable facsimile of true blood. What's it really made of?

Cells, for one.

Red blood cells (a.k.a. erythrocytes) give blood its characteristic red color. These cells are highly specialized (unusual, in other words) in that they have no nucleus. They do contain a lot of hemoglobin, though, and that's what matters when it comes to transporting oxygen.

White blood cells are also there in the blood. They don't contain hemoglobin, because they have an entirely different job: to protect the body against invaders like bacteria or any foreign molecules. During your entire life, as your psyche goes through periods of figuring out just who you are, your white blood cells act out their own identity search on a molecular level, continually distinguishing what is "self" from "nonself." Any molecular, cellular, or substance that your white blood cells can recognize as belonging to your body, it considers "self" and leaves alone. Anything that does not exhibit some familiar cue (in the form of special identity molecules), or that exhibits foreign molecules, the white cells label "nonself" and go after. This search-and-destroy mission is what keeps you healthy in a world full of potential microscopic killers. Pretty amazing, when you think about it.

The blood contains other stuff, too.
Platelets are bits and pieces of cell membrane that help the blood to clot when it needs to (it would be a real drag to bleed to death from a paper cut, so the body tends to make sure that the blood can coagulate, congeal, clot up, in an emergency).

Plasma is the liquid portion of blood; it's a mix of water, ions, dissolved gases, protein, and anything else being transported at the time.

TRADING CARGO AT A CAPILLARY

Let's zero in on a capillary deep in the body tissues. Blood in this capillary has already traveled from the lungs to the right atrium, then the left ventricle, then the aorta, and arterioles to get to this capillary. Once blood reaches this spot, important stuff like oxygen, nutrients, and molecules like hormones can diffuse from the capillaries into the tissues. At the same time, waste products like carbon dioxide can diffuse from the tissues into the capillary.

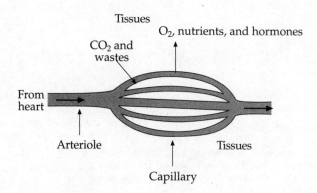

Now that the capillary's blood is minus the good stuff and carries the tissues' waste products, what happens next?

The Return Trip to the Heart

Blood leaves the capillaries through the *venules*, which combine to become *veins* before long. Veins are these stretchy, accommodating blood vessels equipped with *valves* so that blood does not flow backwards by mistake. Instead, blood flows through the veins from the rest of the body back to the heart.

While the blood flowing through the arteries relies on the heart to generate flow pressure, the veins instead rely on your muscle action to keep blood moving. That's why, if you sit too long in one position, your blood tends to pool, causing some stiffness when you get up.

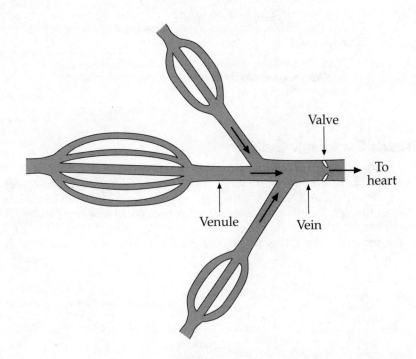

At the heart, the *vena cava* delivers the deoxygenated blood (blood without much oxygen) to the right atrium. When the right atrium contracts, it squeezes the blood through a valve into the right ventricle. The right ventricle contracts and squeezes the blood out through the pulmonary artery, a vessel that takes the blood to the lungs.

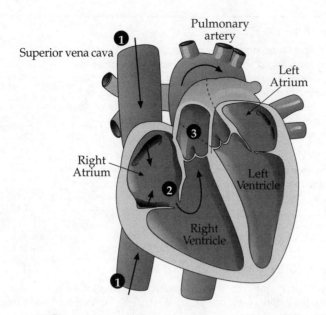

1 blood from body enters right atrium through vena cava

2 the right atrium contracts, squeezing blood to right ventricle

3 the right ventricle contracts, squeezing blood through pulmonary

At capillaries in the lungs, the blood dumps carbon dioxide and picks up oxygen (both by diffusion, as we have said). Now oxygenated blood (blood carrying lots of oxygen) travels from the lungs through the pulmonary vein to the left atrium of the heart, and we're back where we started from.

A QUICK RECAP

There, we've wrapped up all the loose ends. Now let's sketch a quick outline of blood flow, starting with the right atrium of the heart:

from heart: left atrium → left ventricle

towards body tissues: → aorta → arteries → arterioles → capillaries

back towards heart: → venules → veins → vena cava → right atrium → right ventricle

to lungs: → pulmonary artery → lungs

back to heart: → pulmonary vein → left atrium

Connect all the arrows and you've just traced a major pathway of blood flow.

A PICTURE FRAME IS ONLY PART OF THE WHOLE

We've outlined the basic *systemic* (body) and *pulmonary* (lung) circulation routes here. The blood actually follows far more detailed patterns. For instance, the blood makes a special stop at the liver, to drop off some nutrients it picked up from capillaries at the intestines. Blood also has to be supplied to the brain, the lungs themselves, and the heart itself. You get the idea—the picture is a whole lot bigger, but our focus is on just the central view.

THE LYMPHATIC SYSTEM

Lymph is a colorless, watery fluid that travels through the lymph vessels. These are separate from the blood vessels. Lymph contains white blood cells, which should clue you in on one of the lymph system's jobs: it provides immune function, protecting the body from invading organisms. Clusters of white blood cells tend to concentrate in *lymph nodes* found throughout your body. The other important job the lymph system has is in regulating fluid balance. It collects fluid from the tissues and brings it to the blood.

CHECK YOUR PROGRESS 2

1. Name four components of blood.

    1. _____

    2. _____

    3. _____

    4. _____

2. Which is narrower, a venule or a vein?

   _____

3. Which is narrower, an artery or an arteriole?

   _____

4. Which of the following possess valves?

   I. Chambers of the heart
   II. Arteries
   III. Veins

   A. I only
   B. II only
   C. I and II only
   D. I and III only

5. Through which blood vessel does diffusion of nutrients, oxygen, and waste materials take place?

   A. The aorta
   B. The arteriole
   C. The capillary
   D. The venule

6. Which of the following correctly lists the order in which blood travels through the heart?

   A. Aorta, capillaries, arterioles, left ventricle, venules, veins, right ventricle, right atrium, lungs, right atrium
   B. Right atrium, right ventricle, arterioles, capillaries, aorta, venules, veins, left atrium, left ventricle, lungs
   C. Left ventricle, aorta, arterioles, capillaries, venules, veins, right atrium, right ventricle, lungs, right atrium
   D. Left atrium, left ventricle, lungs, aorta, arterioles, capillaries, venules, veins, right atrium, left ventricle

7. All of the following blood vessels carry blood away from the heart EXCEPT

   A. a venule
   B. the aorta
   C. an artery
   D. an arteriole

Refer to the answer choices listed below in answering questions 8-12.

O = oxygenated

D = deoxygenated

8. Blood found within a venule _____

9. Blood found within an arteriole _____

10. Blood leaving the left ventricle _____

11. Blood entering the right atrium _____

12. Blood entering the left atrium _____

THE EXCRETORY SYSTEM

We've talked about how tissues generate carbon dioxide, which gets excreted through the lungs. Well, cells also produce other wastes as a byproduct of their everyday activities—stuff like *salts* and *urea*. These wastes also get carried away from the tissues by the blood, but they don't go to the lungs. A small amount gets excreted by sweat glands in the skin, but most of the waste is destined for the *kidneys*.

You have two kidneys, a left one and a right one. These are connected to *ureters*, which lead to the *bladder*. *Urine* produced by the kidneys gets sent through the ureters to the *bladder*. The urine is temporarily stored there until it is excreted through the *urethra* to the outside of the body.

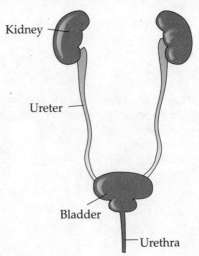

Kidney

Ureter

Bladder

Urethra

Now for a Closer Look

If we took a microscopic look at a kidney, we'd see loads of individual units called *nephrons*. A nephron looks like this:

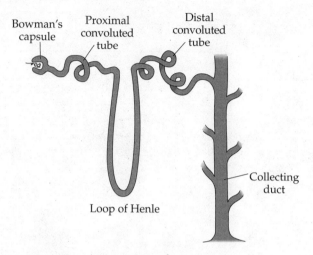

Comings and Goings at the Nephron

Here's how a nephron works. An artery leading to the kidney branches into an arterioles which end in capillaries. You know all of that already. Now we'll look at the bunch of capillaries found at one nephron. The capillaries are collectively called the *glomerulus*, and they're semisurrounded by the *Bowman's capsule*. From the glomerulus, things in the blood get filtered through the Bowman's capsule. What sorts of things? Aside from salts and urea, stuff like water, amino acids, and glucose.

These filtered materials now travel through the nephron, through the *proximal convoluted tubule*, along the *loop of Henle*, and through the *distal convoluted tubule*. As they travel through the nephron, some stuff gets *resorbed* (taken back) from the nephron's interior back into the tissues. What remains in the fluid by the end portion of the nephron is now urine. The urine heads out of the nephron through a *collecting duct*. All collecting ducts lead to the *ureter*. From there, you know the rest: the urine heads to the bladder and out the *urethra*.

It's In the Job Description

The kidneys don't just take care of waste products, which would be dangerous to the body if they were allowed to accumulate. Because the kidneys can adjust how much water and other material should be retained by the body and how much should be thrown out, they act to maintain water, salt, and chemical balances within the body. This vital work falls under the job title homeostasis. Homeostasis is all about keeping things at a steady state inside the body.

---

1. Name three organs that have excretory functions.

    1._____

    2._____

    3._____

Questions 2-6 refer to the diagram below. First fill in the blanks in the diagram with the appropriate terms, and then answer the questions that follow, choosing from among the terms as your answer choices.

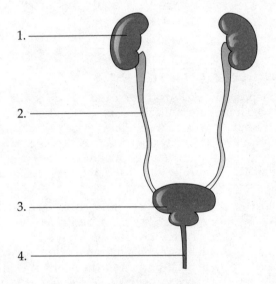

1. ——————

2. ——————

3. ——————

4. ——————

2. Serves as temporary storage for urine

    _____

3. Transports urine to temporary storage area

    _____

4. Conducts urine to the outside of the body

_____

5. Each contains over a million nephrons

_____

6. Removes waste products from the blood and helps to maintain fluid balance _____

7. All of the following are parts of a nephron EXCEPT
   A. the Bowman's capsule
   B. the proximal convoluted tubule
   C. the ureter
   D. the loop of Henle

8. What part of the nephron filters blood from the glomerulus? _____

9. Which of the following take place in the nephron?
   A. Filtration only
   B. Resorption only
   C. Both filtration and resorption
   D. Neither filtration nor resorption

THE DIGESTIVE SYSTEM

We bet you've heard the phrase, "you are what you eat." In a sense, that's true. Whatever you eat gets processed by your body, and whatever basic materials your body finds useful, it incorporates somewhere. We'll show you what we mean.

Since we're heterotrophs, we have to eat things in order to obtain our protein, fats, sugars, vitamins. . .you get the picture. When we eat food, our digestive tract breaks it down into simpler building blocks (like amino acids) that it can actually use.

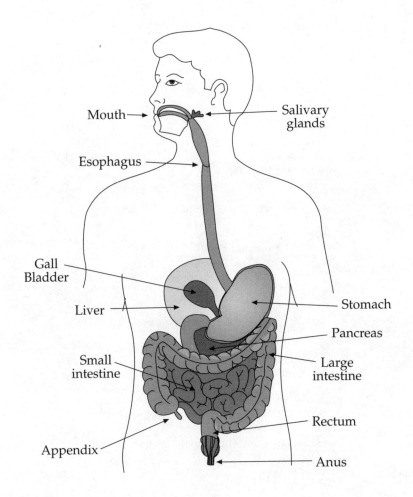

Mouth

Salivary glands

Esophagus

Gall Bladder

Liver

Stomach

Pancreas

Small intestine

Large intestine

Appendix

Rectum

Anus

THE MOUTH

The first step in the breakdown process is chewing our food with our teeth. The tongue helps to move the food around, and the *salivary glands* get into the act, too: they supply saliva. All this chewing action creates a lot of surface area on the food so that digestive enzymes can get at them.

FYI

With the release of saliva enters our first digestive enzyme: *amylase*. Amylase digests starch.

THE ESOPHAGUS

Next the chewed-up food gets swallowed and finds itself in the *esophagus*. Muscles in the esophagus work out to create *peristalsis*, which is a series of contractions that push food down the esophagus and into the stomach. (Peristalsis also keeps the food moving along the rest of the digestive tract.)

THE STOMACH

In the *stomach* some serious mechanical breakdown gets going. There are circular muscles and longitudinal muscles of the stomach, and they work the food over into very small pieces. The stomach takes care of a few other things, too. It stores food (temporarily, of course), and some of its cells secrete *pepsin*, an enzyme that digests protein. Now pepsin only works in an acid environment, but the stomach can handle that: it secretes *hydrochloric acid* (HCl), which has a very low pH.

THE SMALL INTESTINE

The small intestine is amazingly long. It's folded up into layers in the abdomen. On the inner surface of the entire small intestine are *villi* (finger-like bumps) and on those are *microvilli*! This increases the surface area of the small intestine dramatically. What's all that surface area for? Absorption. The small intestine's job is to absorb the basic nutrients released by digestion, like amino acids, glucose, fatty acids, and glycerol. (These organic molecules should ring a bell from chapter 2.)

Where Bile Comes From

A digestive juice called bile *is a funny thing, because it's made by the liver but it's stored in the gall bladder. When the time is right, the gall bladder sends the bile right into the small intestine, where the bile breaks fat into smaller pieces (that's known as emulsification). So bile emulsifies fats. Say it once or twice and you'll always remember that.*

Other secretions into the small intestine come from the pancreas. The pancreas produces a few enzymes that finish up digesting the food stuff in the small intestine.

THE LARGE INTESTINE

Now that the ingested food has been thoroughly digested and the usable bits absorbed, the rest enters the large intestine. Water enters the large intestine along with it. Water also leaves the large intestine (is absorbed) as *feces* forms. The feces is stored in the *rectum* and passes outside of the body through the *anus*.

What's feces made of? Mostly water, quite a few bacteria, indigestible stuff like cellulose, and salts, dead cells, and bile pigments. *Diarrhea* (very watery feces) results when the large intestine fails to resorb all that extra water when the feces is being formed. *Constipation* (very dry feces) results when the large intestine resorbs too much water.

One more note about the large intestine. The *appendix* is a little finger-like dead end off of the large intestine. What does the appendix do? Nothing. Sometimes it gets infected, which is called *appendicitis*, and gets removed by a surgeon.

CHECK YOUR PROGRESS 4

Questions 1-5 refer to the answer choices listed below.

    A. Liver
    B. Pancreas
    C. Stomach
    D. Small intestine

1. Produces bile_____

2. Secretes pepsin _____

3. Site of mechanical digestion_____

4. Secretes digestive enzymes into the small intestine

5. Site of absorption of digested products _____

6. pH is low inside the stomach due to the secretion there of _____   _____.

7. The enzyme pepsin is active only under [acidic _____ basic_____] conditions.

8. Which of the following enzymes is secreted by the salivary glands of the mouth?

   A. Amylase
   B. Pepsin
   C. Lipase
   D. Maltase

9. In which digestive structure is protein initially broken down?

   A. The mouth
   B. The esophagus
   C. The stomach
   D. The small intestine

10. In which digestive structure is starch initially broken down?

    A. The mouth
    B. The esophagus
    C. The stomach
    D. The small intestine

11. Water is absorbed back into the body in which section of the digestive tract?

    The _____

12. Where is bile stored?

    A. In the liver
    B. In the pancreas
    C. In the gall bladder
    D. In the small intestine

13. What is the name given to the series of muscle contractions that push food through the digestive tract? _____

14. Villi are present on which structure of the digestive tract? _____

GLOSSARY

alveolus
(a.k.a. air sac) site of gas exchange in respiration

amylase
enzyme secreted by the salivary glands; digests starch

anemia
deficiency of hemoglobin in red blood cells

anus
opening through which feces passes to the outside of the body

aorta
large artery leading from the left ventricle of the heart to the rest of the body

appendicitis
inflammation of the appendix

appendix
a small tube that originates from the large intestine; no known function in humans

arteries
carry oxygenated blood away from the heart to the rest of the body

arterioles
small blood vessels that arise off of arteries; carry blood away from the heart

atria
(left and right) upper chambers of the heart; separated from one another

bile
digestive juice produced by the liver and stored in the gall bladder; emulsifies fats

bronchi
part of the airway; ringed with cartilage; branch into left and right

bronchioles
numerous branched structures off of the bronchi; part of the airway; lead to the alveoli

capillaries
very narrow blood vessels located in the tissue; site of exchange of materials from the blood and tissues

cartilage
a type of flexible connective tissue; found in trachea, bronchi, and bronchioles

closed circulatory system
    a system of blood vessels designed to transport blood without direct contact
    of blood with the rest of the body

diaphragm
    muscle that helps ventilate the lungs

emulsify
    to break up fat into smaller pieces

erythrocytes
    red blood cells

esophagus
    part of the digestive tract; produces peristalsis; moves food into stomach

expiration
    the act of breathing out during respiration

feces
    produced in the large intestine; composed of undigested wastes

gall bladder
    accessory structure of the digestive system; stores bile

hemoglobin
    a protein found in red blood cells; transports oxygen

homeostasis
    the art of maintaining an even balance of everything within the body, like
    heart rate, fluid balance, etc.

hydrochloric acid
    (a.k.a. HCl) acid secreted by cells of the stomach; lowers pH of stomach
    contents

inspiration
    the act of drawing air into the airways during respiration

large intestine
    section of the digestive tract; resorbs water; feces formed here

liver
    organ that produces bile; also stores glycogen, a concentrated form of
    glucose

lymph
    tissue fluid found within lymph vessels; contains WBCs; serves immune
    function

lymph nodes
    sections of the lymph system where WBCs tend to accumulate to fight
    infection

open circulatory system
a system for transporting blood that allows blood to come into direct contact with the body tissues

pancreas
accessory structure of the digestive system; produces enzymes that it secretes into the small intestine

pepsin
enzyme secreted by the stomach cells; digests protein; works in acid environment

peristalsis
series of muscle contractions that propel food through the digestive tract

plasma
the liquid portion of blood; composed of ions, water, dissolved gases, protein, hormones, etc.

platelets
fragments of cell membrane that help the blood to clot

rectum
section of large intestine that stores feces

red blood cells (RBCs)
found in blood; contain hemoglobin which transports oxygen

salivary glands
located in mouth; secrete saliva, which contains amylase

small intestine
section of digestive tract; site of absorption of nutrients

stomach
muscular organ of the digestive tract; mechanically churns food; cells lining the stomach secrete pepsin and HCl

trachea
upper section of the airway leading to the bronchi; contains cartilage rings

vena cava
two large veins that bring blood from body to right atrium

ventricles
the lower chambers of the heart; pump blood out of the heart

villi
finger-like projections of the small intestine; increases surface area

white blood cells (WBCs)
part of the immune system; help to fight off infection from bacteria and other foreign material

ANSWER KEY

Check Your Progress 1

1. C

2. D

3. the diaphragm

4. A

5. B

6. oxygen molecules diffuse from the capillaries to the body tissues; carbon dioxide molecules diffuse from the body tissues to the capillaries

7. it is expired (exhaled)

Check Your Progress 2

1. red blood cells; white blood cells; platelets; and plasma

2. venule

3. arteriole

4. D

5. C

6. C

7. A

8. D

9. O

10. O

11. D

12. O

Check Your Progress 3

1. the lungs; the skin; the kidneys

2. bladder

3. ureter

4. urethra

5. kidney

6. kidney

7. C

8. the Bowman's capsule

9. C

Check Your Progress 4

1. A

2. C

3. C

4. B

5. D

6. hydrochloric acid

7. acidic

8. A

9. C

10. A

11. large intestine

12. C

13. peristalsis

14. small intestine

12

Human Physiology II

THE NERVOUS SYSTEM, ENDOCRINE SYSTEM, REPRODUCTIVE SYSTEM, AND MUSCULOSKELETAL SYSTEM

When someone taps you on the shoulder, you look up. When you register that it's your best friend, you smile. When he says, "Let's go for pizza around the corner," you get up to go, and your stomach starts growling in anticipation. Naturally during this scene you're not thinking about how you manage to take in information that is at once physical, visual, and auditory, or how you manage to consider the offer and then act on it with the motor coordination necessary to propel you out of your seat and down the street.

You owe your seemingly effortless interactions with the world to your nervous system. Together with the endocrine, the musculoskeletal, and other systems, the nervous system allows you a full range in interpreting stimuli and responding to them. In this chapter we'll find out just how these systems do their jobs. We'll start with how your nervous system manages to coordinate endless incoming information and responses while your mind is strictly on pizza.

THE NERVOUS SYSTEM

STRUCTURE OF A NERVE CELL

The simplest unit of the nervous system is the *nerve cell* (a.k.a. *neuron*). Neurons contain all of the usual organelles found in eukaryotic cells. (Remember chapter 5?) Since neurons are specialized cells, however, they also have some extra features. We'll show you what we mean.

If you were microscopic in size and happened to be walking by a neuron, you might first notice its *dendrites*. Dendrites are finger-like projections of the nerve cell. Next you would pass by the neuron's *cell body*, which houses many organelles and the nucleus. Finally, you would arrive at the neuron's *axon*, a long, arm-like extension coming off of the cell body.

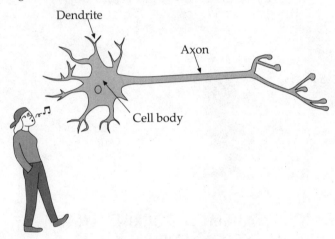

The dendrites, cell body, and axon together make up a nerve cell. The cell membrane surrounds the entire nerve cell.

NEURONS KNOW HOW TO NETWORK

Now, neurons are not solitary cells. They are always found in the company of other neurons. Therefore, if you were to keep on walking—beyond the axon of the neuron you just passed—you would encounter a small space, called a *synapse*, and then you would come upon the dendrites of a second neuron.

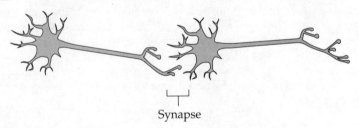

Synapse

Walk past *those* dendrites, *that* cell body, and *that* axon, past *that* synapse, and you may encounter yet another neuron. By now you probably see a pattern emerging here. Neurons always line up from the axon of neuron 1 to the dendrites of neuron 2. In between each neuron is a little space that's called the synapse.

WHAT DOES A NEURON DO?

A neuron is like a busy switchboard operator who picks up and sends out signals. An important thing to remember about this signaling business is that the flow of information is only in one direction. This way signals don't get mixed up. Dendrites always pick up information, and axons always send out information.

Neurons pass information from one cell to the next in the same way that they're lined up: always from the axon of one neuron to the dendrites of the next neuron.

CHECK YOUR PROGRESS 1

1. Fill in the correct terms for the parts of a neuron in the figure provided below.

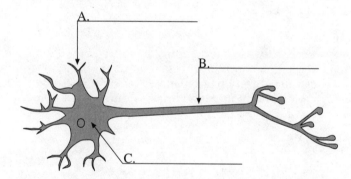

2. The _____ of a neuron sends information out of the cell.

3. A neuron's dendrites _____ information.

4. The flow of information through a nerve cell always occurs in a direction from that cell's

   A. cell body to its dendrites
   B. axon to its cell body
   C. dendrites to its axon
   D. axon to its dendrites

5. The flow of information between two nerve cells always occurs in a direction from the _____ of the first neuron to the_____ of the second neuron.

6. The _____ is actually a space between the axon of one neuron and the dendrites of a second neuron.

DIFFERENT NEURONS HAVE DIFFERENT JOBS

While all neurons relay information, who they get it from and who they relay it to determines what type of neuron they are. There are three types of neurons.

Sensory Neurons

One type of neuron hangs out at a *sensory cell*—like one in the ear, for instance, which registers sound. The neuron that synapses on (forms a connection with but doesn't physically touch) the sensory cell is called a *sensory neuron*. The sensory neuron's dendrites are positioned at the ear's sensory cell in order to quickly pick up any information coming from the sensory cell. The sensory neuron is like a reporter who's waiting to get a story right at the front lines.

Interneurons

What does the sensory neuron do with the information once it gets it? It passes the information on to the next neuron in line. That neuron is sandwiched between the sensory neuron and yet another neuron. It's called an *interneuron*, or *association neuron*, and its job is simply to pass information to the next neuron in line. So far then, we have the following set-up:

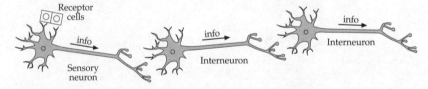

There can be many, many interneurons stationed along a nerve pathway or there can be just a few. In either case, the final interneuron—the one at the end of the line—still has to send its information along to another player. The central nervous system (CNS) is the final destination of the information carried through the neurons.

FYI

The *brain* (a serious concentration of neurons) and the *spinal cord* (which is connected to the brain and contains interneurons) make up the *central nervous system*.

Effector Neuron

Once the information is brought to the CNS, the CNS decides how to respond to it. After the CNS receives a message from an interneuron, it may send another message out through another neuron or set of neurons. The message may go to a muscle (to tell it to contract, for instance), or a gland (to tell it to release a hormone, for instance). The neuron that conveys a message from the CNS to any target that reacts—like a muscle, gland, or organ—is called an *effector neuron*.

MOTOR NEURONS

A *motor neuron* is a special kind of effector neuron. It's message goes straight to a muscle cell.

The Knee-Jerk Response vs. Thinking

A reflex arc is an arrangement of neurons that allows you to have an automatic response to a stimulus, like when your knee jerks in response to a doctor's tap. The simplest reflex arc in the body involves a single sensory neuron and a single motor neuron. (If this were a telephone system, the repair person would have an easy job.)

Thought, on the other hand, is not brought about by a reflex arc. It involves a more complicated arrangement of neurons. In fact, the human brain has 100 billion neurons— give or take a few—that make up to 100 trillion connections among themselves. (A repair job here would be a real headache!)

CHECK YOUR PROGRESS 2

For questions 1-4, match the neuron type listed below with its proper role in transmitting information.

     I. Interneuron
    II. Motor neuron
   III. Effector neuron
   IV. Sensory neuron

1. Receives information from a sensory neuron and transmits it to other neurons _____

2. Relays information from the central nervous system to a muscle cell _____

3. Receives information from a sensory cell _____

4. Transmits information from the central nervous system to a gland, organ, or muscle, producing a response _____

5. The central nervous system consists of the _____ and the _____ _____.

Making Sense of the Nervous System, Nerves, and Neurons

The terms used to describe the nervous system can be confusing. Whole pathways made up of lots and lots of nerve cells form parts of the nervous system, like the central nervous system and the peripheral nervous system.

Zoom in a little closer on the nervous system and you will find nerves—bundles of axons that are concentrated together from many nerve cells. (When someone says to you, "Wow, the nerve in my tooth is starting to act up," she is referring to a bunch of nerves that carry a message from that tooth to his brain.)

Zoom in even closer and follow one axon to its dendrites and cell body, and you isolate a neuron, the basic functional unit of the nervous system.

A Closer Look

Now that we know how neurons connect with one another, we can look at how they get things done. We said that neurons pick up and transmit information. Well, just how do they do that? And what, exactly, do we mean by "information"? These are the sort of thoughts that should be going through your head as you study biology.

Sensory Input

Let's revisit the sensory cell we mentioned earlier. We said it was located in the ear. When sound waves enter the ear, their vibrations cause microscopic hairlike things to flatten on the sensory cell. The sensory cell now stimulates the nearby sensory neuron.

FYI

All sorts of sensory cells are connected with sensory neurons. In the eyes there are *rod* and *cone* cells, which allow vision; in the nose, *olfactory* cells, which allow the sense of smell; on the skin and in the muscles, touch receptors, pain receptors...you get the picture.

THE RESTING NEURON

Depending on when you encounter it, a nerve cell may be resting or it may be busy. A *resting neuron* has no nerve impulses that are passing through it just then. (Of course, the cell is hardly lounging around, either—it's still very busy carrying out all of its normal cell-like jobs, like making ATP, and synthesizing protein and all of that.)

TRANSMISSION OF A NERVE IMPULSE—1-2-3

We're going to track down the route of a nerve impulse in three easy steps. The first step tackles its origins; the second its flow across a neuron; and the third its leap to the next neuron in line. Here we go.

1. *Stimulation at the Dendrites*

Let's say that the dendrites of our resting neuron suddenly get hit with a stimulus. The way in which a sensory cell says to a sensory neuron, "listen up, I've got some news for you," is by producing a change in the neuron's permeability to sodium ions. The change is very local—just at the dendrites at this stage. The change in permeability makes sodium enter the cell at the dendrites.

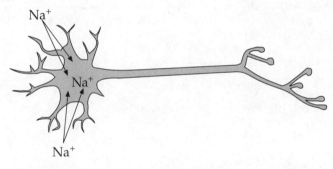

This Side Up

Sodium enters the neuron instead of leaving it because there is a shortage of sodium inside compared to outside, in the tissue fluid. Sodium moves down its concentration gradient, and that means it leaves the extracellular fluid and enters the neuron.

2. *The Action Potential*

So a sensory cell can cause the sensory neuron's membrane to let sodium ions in at the dendrites. What happens next? One of two things:

1. With a weak stimulus, nothing else happens and the stimulus is quickly forgotten.

2. A strong enough stimulus will reach the neuron's *threshold*. What's that? It's the point of stimulation at which a neuron responds with an *action potential*. In an action potential, the entire neuron becomes permeable to sodium ions, and sodium ions rush in across the membrane. Because ions carry charge, this produces an electrical change in the nerve cell's membrane.

It's All or Nothing

A neuron's AP is an all-or-nothing response. The neuron either undergoes an action potential or it doesn't. When this action potential happens the electrical change will spread all the way from the neuron's dendrites to the end of its axon.

An action potential is also called a *nerve impulse*. The impulse is said to be *self-propagating*, because it continues onwards without any help—and without stopping or losing force until it reaches the end of the axon. When the action potential is over, the neuron takes a little time to get back to normal. When it recovers its resting state, its ready for another stimulus.

FYI

1. Once a stimulus reaches threshold in a neuron, it generates an action potential.

2. The action potential is an all-or-nothing response.

3. The action potential is also self-propagating.

4. Eventually the neuron recovers and is ready to respond to a new stimulus.

Check Your Progress 3

1. Stimulation of a neuron [always ___ never _____ sometimes _____] produces an action potential in the neuron.

2. Threshold is defined as the strength of stimulus necessary to provoke in a neuron

   A. a local response, which does not progress past the dendrites
   B. a local response, which does not produce an action potential
   C. an action potential, which travels along the entire neuron
   D. a partial or full action potential, depending on the strength of the stimulus

3. Stimulation of the dendrites increases the neuron's permeability to which one of the following ions?

   A. Sodium
   B. Potassium
   C. Calcium
   D. Hydrogen

4. Which way does sodium flow during an action potential?

   A. Out of the neuron
   B. Into the neuron
   C. Both into and out of the neuron
   D. None of the above

5. Ion flow is associated with electrical _____ .

SALTATORY CONDUCTION

Some neurons conduct nerve impulses faster than other neurons do. The "fast" conductors have something called *myelin sheath* wrapped around their axons. What is a myelin sheath? It's a fatty wrapping around axons provided by a special type of cell. The cell wraps itself around an axon like a jelly roll. In this way it provides insulation for the electrical impulse (caused by the flow of ions) that is charging down the axon.

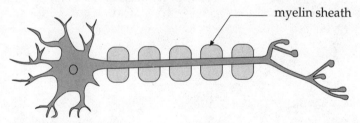

myelin sheath

LEAPFROGGING ACROSS THE NODES OF RANVIER

When an axon is myelinated (wrapped with myelin), an electrical impulse doesn't have to pass through the entire length of the axon; instead the impulse jumps across areas that are not under wraps. These areas of exposed axon are called *nodes of Ranvier*. Because the impulse jumps from node to node, this form of conduction is called *saltatory conduction*, and it's a whole lot faster than on unmyelinated axons.

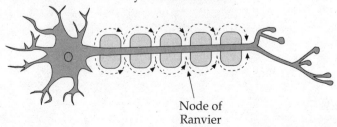

Node of
Ranvier

CHECK YOUR PROGRESS 4

1. The myelin sheath of myelinated axons is composed of [axons _____ cells _____ connective tissue _____].

2. The nodes of Ranvier are [exposed _____ unexposed _____] sections of myelinated axon.

3. Saltatory conduction of a nerve impulse occurs across the [nodes of Ranvier _____ sections of myelin insulation _____].

SYNAPTIC TRANSMISSION

What happens to the action potential once it reaches the end of the axon? It causes small vesicles in the terminal (end) part of the axon to release neurotransmitters into the synapse. Neurotransmitters are "chemical messengers," meaning that they are molecules that help to transmit the nerve impulse. By crossing the synapse and arriving at the neuron across the way, they transmit the nerve impulse from one neuron to the next. Here's how:

1. When an action potential arrives at the terminal end of the axon, it causes synaptic vesicles to fuse with the cell membrane and exocytose what's inside, which happen to be *neurotransmitter molecules*.

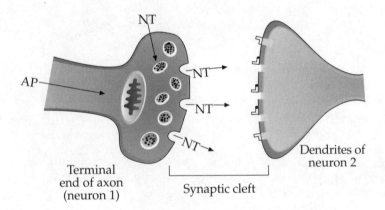

Terminal end of axon (neuron 1)

Synaptic cleft

Dendrites of neuron 2

2. The neurotransmitters travel across the synapse and bind to receptors on the dendrites of the neuron across the way.

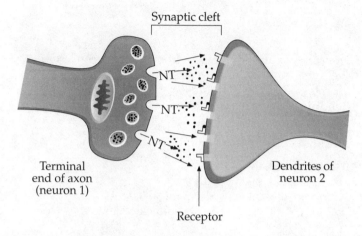

3. When the neurotransmitter binds to this second neuron, it causes the neuron to be more permeable to sodium. That allows sodium ions to flow into the second neuron. If enough sodium flows into the neuron, it triggers an action potential.

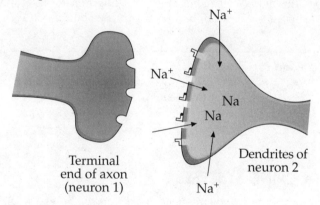

CHECK YOUR PROGRESS 5

1. When a nerve impulse reaches the terminal end of an axon, it causes synaptic vesicles there to fuse with the cell membrane and _____ their contents.

2. Synaptic vesicles at the terminal end of an axon contain [neurotransmitters _____ ions _____ ATP _____], which are released upon arrival of an action potential.

3. Neurotransmitters released from one neuron cross the synapse and bind to [channels _____ receptors _____ pumps _____] located on the dendrites of the next neuron.

4. The transmission of a nerve impulse involves
   A. electrical events only
   B. chemical events only
   C. both electrical and chemical events
   D. neither electrical nor chemical events

A FINAL NOTE ON NEURONS

What is the most important concept that you should walk away with, having finished this section?

We'll tell you: that the nervous system communicates by both *electrical* and *chemical* means. Conduction along a neuron is electrical, because ions move across the nerve cell membrane. Transmission to a second neuron across the synapse is chemical, because neurotransmitters do this job.

Food for Thought

Did you ever think of how many phrases of speech refer to the nervous system? Like, "He's getting on my nerves," and "She's got a lot of nerve," or "You're making me nervous."

THE ENDOCRINE SYSTEM

Working hand in hand with the nervous system is the endocrine system. What makes up the endocrine system? Endocrine glands and the hormones they produce. As you read this, you're likely to have over two dozen different hormones traveling through your blood stream, each headed to specific target cells throughout your body.

What is an Endocrine Gland?

An *endocrine gland* is a tissue that produces a hormone and sends it directly into the blood stream, which we said was an enclosed space. An *exocrine gland*, on the other hand, secretes its products into a duct that leads to the outside of the body. (For instance, the *salivary glands* are an exocrine gland; they secrete saliva into the mouth, an outside space of the body.)

What is a Hormone?

A *hormone* is a chemical that is secreted into the blood stream and acts on a distant target cell. It has some sort of regulatory effect on its target cell.

Hormones—From Head to Toe

Let's look at some endocrine glands and their hormones. We'll start at the head and work our way down the body. Here's our road map:

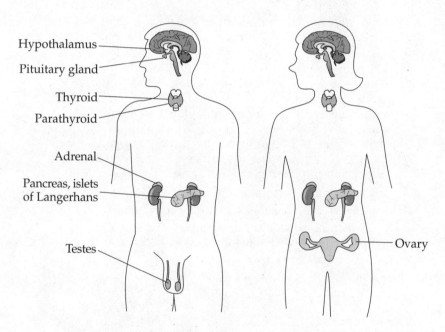

One thing you probably noticed right off from the illustration is that we need to consider females and males differently at some point in our endocrine discussion. When we talked about the heart, the lungs, the kidneys, and other systems, we didn't need to draw a distinction between males and females. With certain glands of the endocrine system, we do. We'll see why when we get to the male and female reproductive glands.

THE HEAD

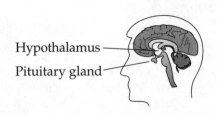

Hypothalamus

Pituitary gland

1. *The hypothalamus*—Right inside the brain is a small area called the hypothalamus. The hypothalamus secretes some hormones that regulate the pituitary gland. The hypothalamus also produces these two hormones, which are stored in the pituitary:

   - *ADH (antidiuretic hormone)*—makes urine more concentrated
   - *oxytocin*—makes the uterus contract during labor, and allows milk to flow in the mammary glands

2. *The pituitary gland*—This gland (also found in the brain) secretes a whole slew of hormones. Some of the hormones in turn control other endocrine glands. An important pituitary hormone is *growth hormone*, which causes the body to grow. Too much GH produces a body that is very big (gigantism); too little GH produces a body that is very small (dwarfism). Here are two other important pituitary gland hormones:

   - *FSH (follicle-stimulating hormone)*—prompts the sex glands (you'll soon encounter) into action
   - *TSH (thyroid-stimulating hormone)*—prompts the thyroid gland to make thyroxine

THE NECK

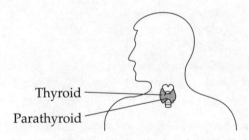

Thyroid

Parathyroid

3. *The thyroid gland*—This gland secretes the hormone *thyroxine*, which affects a person's metabolism. A person

needs thyroxine in order to grow normally. What's more, it has to be the right amount of thyroxine. Too little, and a person can become sluggish. Too much thyroxine makes a person thin, jumpy, and irritable. TSH (thyroid-stimulating hormone, from the pituitary) causes the thyroid to make thyroxine.

Why Salt Supplies Iodine

Your thyroid gland needs iodine in order to produce thyroxine. That's why table salt comes with added iodine.

---

4. *The parathyroid glands*—These glands, found in the thyroid, make parathyroid hormone. What's its job? To increase the amount of calcium that's circulating in the blood. Your body needs calcium for obvious things like bones and teeth, and it also needs calcium for less obvious stuff, like proper muscle and nervous system function.

AROUND WAIST-LEVEL

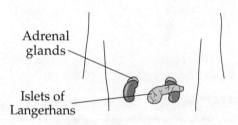

Adrenal glands

Islets of Langerhans

5. *The adrenal glands*—One adrenal gland lies on top of each of your kidneys. If you look closely at the adrenal gland, you'd see an inner and an outer section to it. The inner section is called the *medulla*, and it secretes the hormones *epinephrine* and *norepinephrine* when you're under stress.

The outer section of an adrenal gland is called the *cortex*; it secretes steroid hormones (like *glucocorticoids*) when you're stressed. Steroid hormones help to reduce inflammation and they raise the amount of glucose circulating in the blood stream. Another hormone of the adrenal cortex steps up the amount of sodium and chloride that's absorbed back by the kidney's nephrons. Water follows by osmosis. The result? More concentrated urine and higher blood pressure.

Epinephrine (a.k.a. *adrenaline*) and norepinephrine are called "flight-or-fight" hormones because they gear your body for action: you breathe faster, and your heart pumps faster. Circulation to your skin and digestive system slows down while at the same time blood supply to your muscles, brain, and heart cranks up. The novel-writers may not know it, but this hormone is the reason why their heroines turn pale when they're confronted with something upsetting.

6. *The islets of Langerhans*—You won't find these little islands dotting the St. Lawrence seaway, plunked somewhere in the Puget Sound, or even hugging the New England coastline. They're clusters of cells that exist within the pancreas. These endocrine cells secrete the hormones *insulin* and *glucagon*. Insulin makes the cells take up glucose from the blood stream. That means that the blood will contain less glucose when insulin is around (and the cells will have more glucose). Glucagon, on the other hand, acts to increase the amount of glucose in your blood. It tells the liver to break down some of the glycogen it's storing. Glycogen is dismantled into glucose and sent into the blood stream.

Notice that insulin and glucagon have opposite effects? Insulin lowers blood glucose levels and glucagon *raises* blood glucose levels.

Many of the hormones we looked at have some role in adjusting glucose levels in the blood stream. This should tip you off to how important glucose really is to your body. It constitutes fuel for all the cells in your body, including your brain cells. Its concentration in your blood stream is continually monitored and finely adjusted by way of the hormones we talked about.

Around Hip-Level

7. *The ovaries*—Now we walk through a door that says "in females only." The ovaries are the female gonad, or sex gland. The ovaries secrete a bunch of hormones that help to regulate entire events like the menstrual cycle, pregnancy, and development at puberty. One ovarian hormone—*estrogen*—causes the sex organs and the body to grow during puberty. It also stimulates development of the *secondary sex characteristics*. This means that a female's breasts grow, her pelvis gets wider, and she begins to store fat in specific areas of her body.

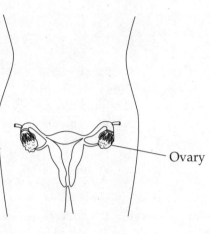

Ovary

The Groin

8. The *testes*—Here we enter the door marked, "in males only." The testes are the male gonad, and they secrete the hormone *testosterone*. This hormone kicks in at puberty, causing the male reproductive organs to grow and the secondary sex characteristics to develop. This means that a guy's voice deepens, his muscles start to develop, and he grows body and facial hair.

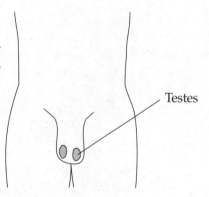

Testes

Check Your Progress 6

1. Which of the following sets of hormones act antagonistically (oppositely) to one another?

   A. Epinephrine and norepinephrine
   B. Glucagon and insulin
   C. Adrenaline and epinephrine
   D. TSH and thyroxine

2. Where are the islets of Langerhans located?

   A. In the thyroid gland
   B. In the parathyroid glands
   C. On top of the kidneys
   D. In the pancreas

3. Epinephrine and norepinephrine, secreted by the adrenal medulla in response to stress, have all of the following effects EXCEPT

   A. they increase blood flow to the heart and the muscles
   B. they decrease blood flow to the digestive system
   C. they increase the heart rate and the respiration rate
   D. they increase blood flow to the skin

4. What is the job of parathyroid hormone, secreted by the parathyroid glands? _____

5. Which of the following is necessary in order for the thyroid gland to produce thyroxine?

   I. FSH
   II. TSH
   III. Iodine

   A. I only
   B. III only
   C. II and III only
   D. I, II, and III

6. Which endocrine gland secretes growth hormone (GH)? _____

7. What hormones are responsible for growth of the reproductive organs and the secondary sex characteristics?

In females: _____

In males: _____

8. Someone has just eaten a big meal (two helpings of everything) and his digestive system has been bravely tackling it. It reaches his small intestine, where (we're sure you remember from chapter 11) nutrients get absorbed into the blood stream. Which hormone is going to kick in any minute now as a result?

   A. Growth hormone
   B. Insulin
   C. Glucagon
   D. Follicle-stimulating hormone

9. A well-known chef has generously offered to teach a class of 200 apprentice chefs how to make her signature soufflé. By the time she is through 7 hours later, she realizes she hasn't had a bite to eat since sun-up. Luckily for her, 200 soufflés are cooling on wire racks. Which hormone is most likely circulating in her blood stream until she manages to eat?

   A. Estrogen
   B. Thyroid-stimulating hormone
   C. Insulin
   D. Glucagon

THE REPRODUCTIVE SYSTEM

We were rather vague when we talked about the "sex organs" and the "reproductive organs." Here, we're going to get good and specific.

THE FEMALE REPRODUCTIVE SYSTEM

What does the female reproductive tract consist of? Well, let's take a look.

THE OVARIES AND THE FALLOPIAN TUBES

The ovaries, we now know, secrete various hormones. They also produce eggs (ova) that they release during *ovulation*. Ovulation occurs once a month. At ovulation, usually only one egg is released from one ovary. The released ovum travels a tiny

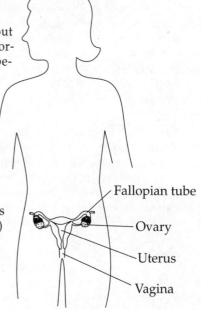

Fallopian tube

Ovary

Uterus

Vagina

distance to the nearby *fallopian tube* (a.k.a. the *oviduct or uterine tube*) and enters it. Once there, it travels the length of the tube. If fertilization is going to happen, it happens in the fallopian tube. Whether it happens or not, the ovum/zygote keeps on traveling until it reaches the *uterus*.

THE UTERUS AND THE VAGINA

The uterus is a muscular organ lined with epithelial cells. That lining has built up in anticipation of a fertilized egg coming its way.

If the Egg Were Fertilized...

...the zygote would implant in the lining of the uterus and grow there, setting up all sorts of accessory structures (like the placenta and the umbilical cord) that would allow an exchange of oxygen and nutrients (Mom's) and wastes (fetus').

Things would move along at a brisk pace developmentally until the fetus was ready to be delivered, about nine months later. At this point, some hormones like oxytocin would kick in, and the uterus would launch a series of powerful contractions. (When we said the uterus was muscular, we weren't kidding.)

Those contractions would propel the fetus through the cervix, down the vagina, and out of the body. The placenta would follow. Labor would then be over, and once the umbilical cord was cut, you would have two newly sepa-rated organisms before you—one large, and one very small. Both would need a big rest.

An *unfertilized* egg doesn't bury itself in the uterus' lining. Instead, the egg keeps moving through the uterus and it's opening (the cervix) and along a passageway (the vagina) to the outside of the body.

MENSTRUATION

What about all that built-up tissue in the uterus? It doesn't hang around to see what the next ovulation brings. Instead it detaches and leaves the body the same way that the egg does: through the vagina to the outside of the body. This monthly shedding of the uterine lining and blood supply is called *menstruation*. It happens when fertilization doesn't, and it lasts any-where from 2 to 7 days. The entire sequence of events is referred to as the *menstrual cycle*, since the whole process of egg maturation, build-up of uterine lining, ovulation, and shedding takes place every 28 days, give or take a few. Don't forget that hormones secreted by the ovaries—with names like *estrogen* and *progesterone*—play a big role in this cycle. Estrogen causes the uterine lining to build up and to lay in a supply of new blood vessels. Progesterone causes the uterine lining to produce nutrients for the zygote, should it arrive. If, however, no zygote shows up, estrogen and progesterone productions plummet, and the built-up tissue of the uterus sloughs off.

THE MALE REPRODUCTIVE SYSTEM

Now let's take a look at the male reproductive tract:

THE TESTES AND THE SCROTUM

Males have two testes. Their job, aside from secreting testosterone, is to produce *sperm cells*, which the male can then deposit into the female's reproductive tract. The testes are housed by the *scrotum*, a sac-like extension from the body that keeps the sperm slightly cooler than the rest of the body. (This minor difference of 2 degrees Celsius can have big consequences— like sterility—if it's altered.)

THE SPERM DUCT, URETHRA, AND PENIS

Newly-made sperm travel through the *vas deferens* (a.k.a. *sperm duct*) and enter the *urethra*. The urethra is a tube that extends through the penis to the outside of the body. While the sperm are passing through these various tubes, a number of other glands are busy adding this and that to the mix. The result is *semen*, a mixture of sperm cells and liquid secretions.

FYI

The penis is a structure specialized for internal fertilization. The vagina serves as a passageway for menstrual flow, as the birth canal, and as a receptacle for sperm deposited by the male.

CHECK YOUR PROGRESS 7

1. The lining of the uterus is shed during which of the following events?

   A. Maturation
   B. Ovulation
   C. Fertilization
   D. Menstruation

2. The structure through which an ovum travels immediately following ovulation is the

   A. fallopian tube
   B. ovary
   C. uterus
   D. vagina

3. Name two structures that are associated with a developing fetus.

   I. _____

   II. _____

4. What structure does sperm travel through after it leaves the testes and before it enters the urethra?

   _____

5. Sperm cells pass out of the body through the

   _____ .

6. What is the main function of the scrotum?

   _____ .

THE MUSCULOSKELETAL SYSTEM

SOME ANIMALS WEAR THEIR SKELETONS ON THEIR SLEEVES

If you were an *arthropod*, like a grasshopper, a dragonfly or a lobster, you'd have an *exoskeleton* (external skeleton). The exoskeleton contains a mix of protein and polysaccharides called *chitin*. Chitin gives the animal that horrible crunch sound when you accidentally step on it. The exoskeleton protects the arthropod's inner organs, provides support, and wards off moisture loss. How can arthropods move around in all that armor? Well, like armor, segments of their exoskeleton are jointed.

THE ENDOSKELETON

Since, of course, you're a *vertebrate* (you possess a backbone) and not an arthropod, you have a different support system for your body—an *endoskeleton* (internal skeleton). What's more, your endoskeleton is not made of chitin—it's made of bone.

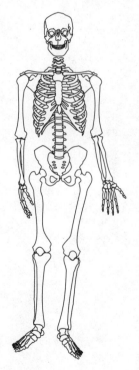

Bone is made up of all sorts of things—like cells, proteins, minerals, and calcium. The inside of bone is called *bone marrow*, and is made of a *spongy tissue*. Now, bone does not only offer support. It also protects your organs, manufactures blood cells (in its marrow), and provides a place for your muscles to attach.

Arthropods have to step out of their exoskeleton every so often, because chitin doesn't grow along with the animal. The arthropods have to abandon their old exoskeleton and grow an entirely new one (that's called *molting*).

Vertebrates, on the other hand, don't have to resort to this—because bone is living tissue, it grows right along with the animal. Bone cells, called *osteoblasts* and *osteoclasts*, are constantly rearranging bone structure on a microscopic scale.

CARTILAGE, TENDONS, AND LIGAMENTS

Like the arthropods, we vertebrates would be in big trouble if we weren't provided with some way to move our inflexible skeleton. Stiff would be an understatement in describing how we'd feel if we had to move our entire skeleton as one rigid piece. Luckily for us our skeleton is equipped with all sorts of joints and connective tissues, which provide us with flexibility. The threesome listed below help to give us our freedom of movement:

1. *Cartilage*—We met up with cartilage in chapter 11, when we looked at parts of the airway. Cartilage also exists here and there among the skeleton, like at your joints. You'll also find it at the tip of your nose and your ear. Give your upper ear a gentle tug and you'll discover that cartilage is quite flexible.

2. *Tendons*—These are not flexible. They connect your muscles to your bones.

3. *Ligaments*—These rate somewhere in between cartilage and tendons on the elasticity scale. You'll find them at all of your movable joints, like your elbow and your knee. They're the hinge that connects the lower part of the bone to the upper part.

WALK MUCH? TALK MUCH?

Whether you've got Swartzeneggar's physique or not, you've got muscles—and plenty of them. Together with your bones, cartilage, tendons and ligaments, they're behind every move you make—from serious athletic endeavors, to mundane stuff like scratching your nose, to indispensable acts, like breathing.

STRIATED MUSCLES

Not all muscles are alike. Some are *striated* (striped), like the ones that attach to your skeleton. Appropriately enough, these are called *skeletal muscles*. You use your skeletal muscles every time you do something intentional, like lift your arms, swing your leg, roll your eyes, or run a race.

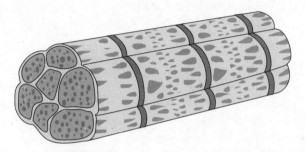

Another type of striated muscle is *cardiac* (a.k.a. *heart*) *muscle*. You don't have any voluntary control over cardiac muscle, which is just as well.

What gives a striated muscle its stripes? Among many other features, striated muscle contains two proteins, named *actin* and *myosin* (a.k.a. *thin* and *thick* filaments). These filaments overlap in certain places, and that's what gives the striated muscle its stripes. The muscle contracts (which is a complicated business) when the actin and the myosin hook up and slide past one another. Muscle contraction requires energy. In fact, the more active a muscle is—like the flight muscle of an insect—the more mitochondria it contains, to supply it with ATP.

SMOOTH MUSCLE

What are *smooth muscles*? Muscles that are not striped. Like striated muscles, smooth muscles also contract, but they're taking care of *involuntary* business. For instance, when we said in chapter 11 how peristalsis worked all along the digestive system, we were speaking of smooth muscles. When we talked of the involuntary contractions of the uterus during labor, we were looking at smooth muscle there, too.

FYI

While it's easy to think of all cells as having a roundish, circular shape, that's not actually true. Different cells have different shapes. Some cells, for example, are cuboidal. Muscle cells, it so happens, are long and thin. That's why we call them muscle *fibers*. Muscles are just bundles of muscle fibers.

CHECK YOUR PROGRESS 8

1. Which of the following is NOT true concerning arthropods?

    A. They have jointed appendages (like legs).
    B. They possess an exoskeleton.
    C. Their skeletal structure is composed mainly of minerals and cells.
    D. Among their ranks are insects and crustaceans such as crabs and lobsters.

2. List 4 things that bone provides for the body.

    1._____

    2._____

    3._____

    4._____

3. Bone is one type of connective tissue that makes up the endoskeleton. What are the three other connective tissue types intimately associated with bone?

    1._____

    2._____

    3._____

4. All of the following are smooth muscles EXCEPT

    A. those in the digestive tract
    B. those in the uterus
    C. those in the diaphragm
    D. those in the heart

5. Name a striated muscle whose contractions are involuntary_____

6. Does muscle contraction require energy?
   yes _____   no _____

7. List two proteins involved in the contraction of skeletal muscle.

   I. _____

   II. _____

8. Which of the following statements about skeletal muscle would you agree with?

   A. It undergoes involuntary contraction.
   B. It is a type of smooth muscle.
   C. It has a striped appearance when viewed under a microscope.
   D. It is composed of cube-shaped cells.

GLOSSARY

Even if you think you already know these terms, or that cleaning your room rates higher on the entertainment scale, look over each word in the glossary. Sometimes you don't realize that a term you're used to seeing around, like *reflex*, has a specific biological meaning. Also, some potentially confusing terms are set straight here, so don't pass them by. Building up your biology vocabulary will do wonders for your understanding of biology—and that gets you higher bio scores.

actin
> (a.k.a. thin filament) a protein found in striated muscle cells; interacts with myosin to produce a contraction

action potential
> (a.k.a. nerve impulse) an electrical flow across a neuron's membrane

ADH (antidiuretic hormone)
> released by the hypothalamus, stored in the pituitary gland until needed; this hormone makes urine more concentrated

adrenal cortex
> outer part of adrenal gland; secretes steroids (such as glucocorticoids) and a hormone that makes urine more concentrated

adrenal gland
> endocrine gland located at top of kidneys; composed of medulla and cortex

adrenal medulla
> inner part of adrenal gland; secretes epinephrine and norepinephrine

arthropod
> animals (including insects and crustaceans) with an exoskeleton made of chitin and having jointed appendages

axon
> long arm-like extension of neuron; transmits information

bone
> component of the endoskeleton; composed of a mix of organic and inorganic material such as cells, collagen, calcium, and minerals

brain
> a large and complex collection of neurons housed in the skull; part of the CNS

cardiac muscle
> a form of striated muscle, its contractions are under involuntary control

cartilage
> a form of connective tissue; flexible and elastic; found in parts of endoskeleton

central nervous system
> made up of the brain and the spinal cord

cervix

(Latin for "neck") the lower section of the uterus; opens to the vagina

chitin

main component of the exoskeleton of arthropods; composed of polysaccharides and protein

dendrites

finger-like projections on a neuron; receive information

effector neuron

transmits information from the CNS to a gland, organ, or muscle, causing a response

endocrine gland

a gland that secretes a product directly into the blood stream (an enclosed space)

endoskeleton

an internal skeleton composed of bone, cartilage, tendons, and ligaments; provides protection and support

epinephrine

(a.k.a. adrenaline) hormone secreted by the adrenal medulla in response to stress; together with norepinephrine increases blood flow to muscles, heart and brain, decreases blood flow to digestive system and capillaries near skin

estrogen

(a.k.a. female sex hormone) hormone secreted by the ovaries in females; spurs development of female reproductive organs and secondary sex characteristics

exoskeleton

hard protective outer skeleton of arthropods; composed chiefly of chitin

fallopian tube

(a.k.a. uterine tube or oviduct) the two fallopian tubes of the female serve as passageways through which the ovum travels towards the uterus; site of fertilization

FSH (follicle-stimulating hormone)

secreted by the pituitary gland; stimulates ova to mature in ovaries of females and sperm to be made in testes of males

glucagon

hormone secreted by the islets of Langerhans; raises blood glucose levels

glucocorticoids

a type of steroid; hormones released by the adrenal cortex; reduce inflammation and increase blood glucose levels

growth hormone (GH)

secreted by the pituitary gland; stimulates the body to grow

hormone
> a substance that is secreted into the blood stream and has a regulatory effect on distant target cells or tissues

hypothalamus
> endocrine gland located in the brain; secretes hormones that regulate the pituitary gland; secrete ADH and oxytocin, which are then stored in the pituitary

interneuron
> sandwiched between two neurons; relays information from one neuron to the next

insulin
> hormone secreted by the islets of Langerhans; lowers blood glucose levels

islets of Langerhans
> endocrine gland composed of small patches of cells located in the pancreas; secrete insulin and glucagon

ligament
> a type of connective tissue that joins bones to one another

menstrual cycle
> an approximately month-long series of events that include the maturation of an ovum, its release from an ovary, the build-up of the uterine lining, and its subsequent sloughing off if the ovum is not fertilized

menstruation
> the sloughing off and discharge of uterine blood and tissue in females

motor neuron
> a neuron that synapses on a muscle; carries information from the CNS to the muscle, causing it to contract

myosin
> (a.k.a. thick filament) a protein found in a striated muscle cell; interacts with actin to produce a contraction

neurotransmitters
> (a.k.a. chemical messengers) molecules that travel across the synapse, transmitting the nerve impulse from one neuron to the next

norepinephrine
> hormone secreted by the adrenal medulla in response to stress; acts in conjunction with epinephrine to produce "fight-or-flight" response

osteoblasts
> a type of bone cell

osteoclasts
> a type of bone cell

ovaries
the female gonad; secrete the hormones estrogen and progesterone; site of ova maturation

ovulation
process by which a mature ovum is released from the ovary; occurs approximately once a month

oxytocin
hormone released by hypothalamus and stored in pituitary; causes uterine contractions during labor and milk to enter mammary duct

parathyroid hormone
secreted by the parathyroid gland; causes calcium level in the blood to rise

penis
male reproductive organ designed for internal fertilization; deposits sperm in the female via the urethra

pituitary gland
endocrine gland located in the brain; secretes growth hormone, FSH, and TSH

reflex
an automatic response to a stimulus due to a specific arrangement of neurons

resting neuron
a neuron that is not undergoing an action potential

scrotum
part of the male reproductive system that encloses the testes; keeps sperm slightly cooler than body temperature

secondary sex characteristics
in females includes such features as development of breasts, pattern of fat storage; in males, deepening of voice, muscle development, and hair growth

semen
a liquid mixture of sperm cells and secretions from various male reproductive glands

sensory cell
a cell that picks up information directly from the environment and transmits it to a sensory neuron

sensory neuron
a nerve cell that synapses on a sensory cell and receives information from the sensory cell

skeletal muscle
attaches to the skeleton; under voluntary control; striated

smooth muscle
> lacks striated appearance; under involuntary control; found in digestive tract, various internal organs

sperm duct
> (a.k.a. vas deferens) tube of the male reproductive tract through which sperm travel to reach the urethra

spinal cord
> continuous with brain; coordinates information between the brain and the rest of the body; contains interneurons

sterile
> unable to successfully fertilize or reproduce

striated muscle
> muscle containing overlapping filaments of actin and myosin, such as skeletal and cardiac muscle

synapse
> a space between two neurons or between a neuron and another cell

synaptic vesicles
> located in the terminal part of the neuron's axon; contain neurotransmitters

tendon
> a type of connective tissue that joins up two muscles or a muscle to a bone

testes
> the male gonad; secretes the hormone testosterone; site of sperm production

testosterone
> (a.k.a. male sex hormone) secreted by the testes in males; causes the male reproductive organs to grow and stimulates development of male secondary sex characteristics

threshold
> the level of stimulation required to trigger an action potential in a neuron

thyroid gland
> endocrine gland located in the neck; secretes thyroxine

thyroxine
> hormone secreted by the thyroid gland; affects metabolism; needed for growth

TSH (thyroid-stimulating hormone)
> secreted by the pituitary gland; causes the thyroid to produce and release thyroxine

uterus
> muscular organ of the female reproductive tract; site of fetal development

vagina
> passageway-like muscular organ of the female reproductive tract; site of sperm deposition; birth canal

ANSWER KEY

Check Your Progress 1

1. A. dendrites; B. axon; C. cell body
2. axon
3. receives
4. C
5. axon; dendrites
6. synapse

Check Your Progress 2

1. I
2. II
3. IV
4. III
5. brain; spinal cord

Check Your Progress 3

1. sometimes
2. C
3. A
4. B
5. charge

Check Your Progress 4

1. cells
2. unexposed
3. nodes of Ranvier

Check Your Progress 5

1. exocytose
2. neurotransmitters
3. receptors
4. C

Check Your Progress 6

1. B
2. D
3. D
4. to increase the amount of calcium in the blood stream
5. C
6. the pituitary gland
7. estrogen; testosterone
8. B
9. D

Check Your Progress 7

1. D

2. A

3. the placenta, the umbilical cord

4. the sperm duct (vas deferens)

5. the urethra

6. to cool the sperm cells to slightly below body temperature

Check Your Progress 8

1. C

2. support; protects the internal organs; produces blood cells; provides site for muscle attachment

3. tendons; ligaments; cartilage

4. D

5. the heart

6. yes

7. actin; myosin

8. C

13

Ecology

ECOLOGY: THE FOOD CHAIN, SYMBIOSIS, SUCCESSION, AND BIOMES

You pretty much know how you fit in in your school, your home, and your neighborhood. But do you know what your *biome* is? Could you identify your *niche*? Are you an *herbivore*, a *carnivore*, or an *omnivore*? What about a *parasite*? Are you on the bottom or the top of the food chain, or somewhere in between? Are you into *symbiosis*? In this chapter, you'll find these things out.

A NICHE OF ONE'S OWN

A niche is an interesting concept, because it does not take into account just one thing. It's not where you live (your habitat), nor is it what you eat (your nutrition) or how you track down your food (foraging). It isn't how much space you need in order to live, to mate, to raise a family, and to get food (your territory). It isn't any one of these things, but it includes all of them. A niche defines an animal's lifestyle. It takes into account everything the animal does and makes use of in order to live. Some closely related types of animals, for instance, can share the same or overlapping spaces because they occupy different niches in that space.

COMPETITION

Closely related to the idea of an organism's niche is *competition*. In the natural world competition is not a staged event held in a stadium and attended by fans, or a face-off by two athletes or two sport teams. Nor, of course, is it a race to see who gets the highest score in math class. In nature, competition has far higher stakes than honor, glory, prize money, or a trophy: survival. The survival is actually twofold: survival of the organism itself, and survival of the organism's genes in future generations.

IT'S A CRUEL WORLD

Animals compete with each other when they share the same niche, or overlapping niches. Competition is a struggle by organisms for the same limited resources, like shelter, food, mates, or territory. An animal that runs faster, jumps higher, locates food quicker, fights stronger, or in some way outperforms other animals that need

the same things in life—will win the competition, because it's more fit. Fitness has to do with how well an organism is able to compete for resources. The losers tend to drop out of the competition—they die. When they die, their genes go with them. The winners—the more fit organisms—keep on living. They have a better chance of reaching reproductive age and producing offspring. That way they keep their genes going in future generations.

About Species

Competition can take place between organisms belonging to the same species, or to different species. A *species* is a group of organisms that has enough genes in common to be able to mate and produce offspring. A *population* is a group within a species who share the same habitat. So there can be different populations within a species, but all members of a species can successfully interbreed.

Producers, Consumers, and Decomposers

We mentioned producers a long time ago in chapter 7. We said that they're autotrophs—they make their own food using energy from sunlight. They're mostly plants, and blue-green algae, plus a few other interesting characters.

Consumers in this context won't be found at the mall. We said that consumers are organisms that have to eat something else in order to get their nutrition. Animals and bacteria are consumers.

Decomposers are a special class of consumers that decompose organisms—right down to an organism's minerals, carbon dioxide, and water. Decomposers are the original recyclers here on Earth, freeing up basic material so that it's available for reuse. Fungi (like mushrooms) are decomposers.

An Appetite for Others

Consumers get named based on their appetites. Carnivores *eat meat.* Herbivores *eat plants.* Omnivores *eat both.* Saprophytes *absorb their food from dead organisms.*

Check Your Progress 1

Questions 1-4 refer to the following answer choices.

    A. Niche
    B. Competition
    C. Fitness
    D. Population

1. Members of a species_____

2. A struggle for the same limited resources _____

3. Takes into account an animal's entire lifestyle ____

4. Influences an animal's ability to compete and to survive to reproductive age _____

5. Occurs when animals' niches overlap _____

6. All of the following are producers EXCEPT

   A. cacti
   B. pea plants
   C. blue-green algae
   D. mushrooms

7. What basic materials do decomposers free up from dead organisms, so that those materials can be used over? _____,_____ , and _____ .

8. A bear foraging for food first swipes open a honeycomb to get at the honey, then feasts on some blueberry bushes, ambles over to a rotten log to search for grubs, and ends up by a stream, eating a salmon it just caught. Based on its diet, the bear is a(n):

   A. omnivore
   B. herbivore
   C. carnivore
   D. saprophyte

THE FOOD CHAIN: WHO EATS WHOM

Now that we know our role players, we can set up the *food chain*. Producers are at the bottom. A step up from them on the food chain are the *primary consumers*, who directly eat the producers. A step up from the primary consumers are the *secondary consumers*. Secondary consumers eat primary consumers. Directly above the secondary consumers are *tertiary consumers*. Tertiary consumers eat secondary consumers. Decomposers don't get pigeonholed in the food chain, because they decompose organisms at every one of its levels.

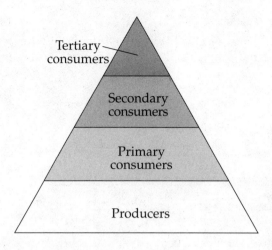

WE'VE ACTUALLY CONSTRUCTED A PYRAMID

A PYRAMID OF NUMBERS

The food pyramid above reveals the relative numbers of organisms at each *trophic* (feeding) *level*. Producers have the most numbers. As you go up, the numbers of organisms keep on getting smaller. This means that in our grassy meadow there will be more rabbits than snakes, and more snakes than hawks. To understand why this is so, we have to look at the energy available in a food chain.

An Energy Pyramid

The amount of energy originally available from the producers as you go up the pyramid shrinks dramatically.

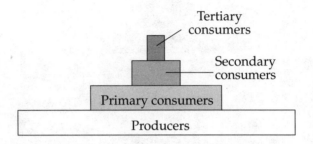

That's because energy is a derivative commodity. Here's what we mean. All of the energy that is available to organisms is created by the producers. As you move up one trophic level—from producers to primary consumers—there's a sharp drop in the amount of energy that's still available for use. Once the primary consumers take and use up some of their energy, even less is available for those at the next trophic level. Finally, a very small amount of the original energy that was available way at the bottom is left for the predator at the top of the food chain.

"It Takes a Village to Raise a Child"

So goes an anthropological saying about the collective work required to support a child's development. Well, when it comes to supporting a *top predator*, it takes the work of the entire rest of the food chain—all of the producers, the other trophic levels, and everyone's collective land requirements. That's why there are so few top predators. The rest of the food chain simply can't afford to support more of them.

Check Your Progress 2

Questions 1 and 2 refer to the scene presented below.

You arrive at a pond just in time to witness a bullfrog gulp up a fly and then a snake swallow the bullfrog.

1. The producer is
   A. the fly
   B. the bullfrog
   C. the snake
   D. none of the above

2. Which organism will have the fewest numbers?

    A. The fly
    B. The bullfrog
    C. The snake
    D. Cannot tell from the information given.

Questions 3-6 refer to the food chain presented below.

marine algae → minnow → mackerel → seal → killer whale

3. The primary consumer is the

    A. marine algae
    B. minnow
    C. mackerel
    D. seal

4. The top predator is the

    A. minnow
    B. mackerel
    C. seal
    D. killer whale

5. Which of the following is true concerning the flow of energy in this food chain?

    A. The minnow has access to more energy than does the mackerel.
    B. The mackerel has access to more energy than does the minnow.
    C. The seal has access to more energy than does the mackerel.
    D. The killer whale has access to the most energy.

6. Which is the producer?

    A. The marine algae
    B. The minnow
    C. The mackerel
    D. None of the above

WHATEVER GETS YOU THROUGH THE NIGHT (AND DAY): SYMBIOSIS

While labels like carnivore and herbivore give us a glimpse into an organism's feeding preferences, there are still more habits to be probed. For instance, the whole topic of *symbiosis* sheds light on some interesting behaviors. Symbiosis means that organisms of two different species share an unusual relationship: they live together. They're on very intimate terms with one another.

EVERYTHING YOU ALWAYS WANTED TO KNOW ABOUT SYMBIOTIC RELATIONSHIPS BUT WERE AFRAID TO ASK

1. *Parasitism*—In parasitism someone gets hurt. Here one organism benefits, but the other one suffers. (Definitely not a good model for one's own relationships.)

EXAMPLES OF PARASITISM

- The heartworm gains access to a canine's heart as tiny larvae transmitted by mosquitoes. There the larvae develop into worms and multiply, clogging up the heart chambers. Without treatment (with arsenic, of all things), a dog parasitized by heartworms will die from a strangled heart.

- Compared to heartworms, fleas are practically benign parasites of canines. They're only out for a little blood.

- Another type of parasitic worm called brainworm, drives moose stark, raving mad before eventually killing them.

- Humans are not exempt either; tapeworms, certain snails, and many other parasites find us very attractive.

2. *Commensalism*—This form of symbiosis is a lot less diabolical than parasitism, but it's still not the ideal relationship role model, if you ask us. Here, one partner benefits, and the other one neither benefits nor suffers.

EXAMPLES OF COMMENSALISM

- The pilotfish is a shark groupie: it hovers close to the shark for stray bits of food. Crumbs that size that mean nothing to the shark, but they serve the pilotfish quite well.

- Epiphytes (air plants) cling high up to the branches of a tree in order to gain anchorage without having to put down their own roots.

3. *Mutualism*—Here behind door number three is the best role model for a relationship of one's own. In mutualism both partners benefit. The saying, "You scratch my back and I'll scratch yours" pretty much sums up this type of relationship.

EXAMPLES OF MUTUALISM

- One type of bacteria hangs out on the root nodules of certain plants. The bacteria get a place to hang their hats (if they had them) and in return they process nitrogen into a form the plant can use. Both the nitrogen-fixing bacteria and the plant are happy with this arrangement.

- Ants and aphids are another case study. The aphids imbibe so much plant juice that most of it passes right through them, relatively unchanged. Waiting at the other end are the ants, who gain access to all that sugar with little effort. What do the aphids get in return? Protection. Any ladybug or fly larvae with an aphid dinner on its mind gets driven off by the ants. Think about that the next time you pass some plant stem with a few bugs on it.

CHECK YOUR PROGRESS 3

1. Which of the following is true regarding symbiosis?

   A. It involves a pairing of organisms of the same species.
   B. Two organisms form a short-lived partnership.
   C. At least one member of the pair always suffers.
   D. At least one member of the pair always benefits.

Questions 2-4 refer to the answer choices listed below.

   I. Parasitism
   II. Mutualism
   III. Commensalism

2. Termites harbor bacteria in their intestines which are able to digest cellulose. That's handy for the termites, since they eat wood. The bacteria in turn receive shelter and protection. What's this form of symbiosis called?

3. Nitrogen-fixing bacteria and the plants they live with have what kind of symbiotic relationship?

   _____

4. A deer tick and a deer represent what kind of symbiotic relationship? _____

5. Commensalism is a symbiotic association in which

   A. one partner is injured and the other benefits
   B. both partners benefit
   C. both partners are injured
   D. one partner benefits and the other neither is helped nor harmed

6. Epiphytes living on trees are an example of which kind of symbiosis?

ECOLOGICAL SUCCESSION

Let's shift gears now and move into habitat. Say you go out for a walk every decade or two. On your first walk, you happen upon a bare field, without any vegetation on it. On your next walk, nearly ten years later, you get to where the bare field should be, only now its an open meadow that is filled with grasses, and a few flowers. When you return to that spot ten years later, you find yet a different environment: shrubland. Gone are the expanses of grasses and flowers and in their place are a lot of low trees and bushes. You return in about another decade to be met with further change: mostly woods exist. Gone are all the shrubs and in their place are evergreen trees, like pine and cedar. On your next walk, two decades later, the evergreens are nowhere in sight, but oak trees, beech trees, and maple trees greet you.

To Drop or Not to Drop

Oak, beech, and maple trees are called deciduous trees, because they drop their leaves every winter. Evergreen trees are called conifers, because they hold on to their leaves during the cold season. (That's why their leaves have been modified into those spiky green needles you see.)

THE CLIMAX COMMUNITY

How long will things keep on changing? Your return visit a decade or two hence surprises you: the oaks, beeches, and maples are *still there*. They won't be replaced by other types of vegetation, because they represent the *climax community*. The climax community consists of plant life that will remain in an area. A climax community is stable, and fairly diverse (has different types of plants in it). Assuming that it doesn't get turned into pavement by human hands, or that a fire or tornado doesn't roar through it, a climax community won't change much.

The climax community represents the final stage of an *ecological succession*. In a succession, plants alter their environment in ways that ironically make it less habitable for them and more inviting to an entirely different group of plants. So around every ten to thirty years, a whole *new* set of plants live in the area, until the climax community of plants settles in. And as the *plant* community in an area keeps changing, the *animal* communities do also. Mice and rabbits live in fields. Deer and bear live in woods. You get the idea.

SOME TYPICAL STAGES OF SUCCESSION

1. bare rock or bare field→ grassland→ shrub→ evergreens→ deciduous trees

2. bare pond → submerged plants → cattails and sedges → grasses→ shrubs→ conifers→ deciduous trees

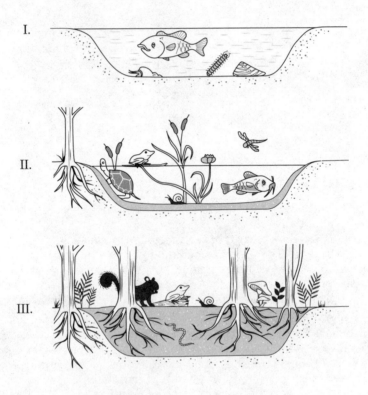

THE PIONEER COMMUNITY

Now that we know about the climax community, let's shift all the way over to the opposite end of succession for a look at the *pioneer community*. The pioneer community is made up of the plant forms that originally colonize an area. They're the first ones there.

Pioneer organisms are a pretty hardy group. What other kind of plant life would take on the challenge, for instance, of colonizing bare rock? *Lichen* has this privilege, blown there by the wind. Actually the product of a symbiotic association of algae and fungi, lichen looks like a big splat of paint on bare rock.

A FOOTNOTE

Students sometimes confuse *succession* with *evolution*. These are two wildly different events. One can be measured in decades (succession), the other must be measured over many generations (evolution). One involves what kinds of plant life move in and out of an area (succession), while the other involves a change in the genetic make-up of a population of organisms (evolution).

CHECK YOUR PROGRESS 4

1. What plant community is the first to colonize a site in an ecological succession? _____

2. What plant community is the last to colonize a site in an ecological succession? _____

3. What plant form is the most likely to colonize bare rock?
   A. Lichen
   B. Algae
   C. Grasses
   D. Shrubs

4. Which of the following is correct concerning a typical ecological succession?
   A. A conifer forest will be replaced by a deciduous forest.
   B. A deciduous forest will be replaced by a conifer forest.
   C. Shrubs and bushes will be replaced by grasses.
   D. Grasses will be replaced by bare field.

5. Draw in the stages of succession from a bare field to a climax community in the figure shown below.

Bare field | Grasses | Shrubs | Conifer forest | Deciduous forest

6. The final outcome in the ecological succession of a pond is a

   A. grassland
   B. bare rock
   C. forest
   D. lake

BIOMES

Succession involves habitat on a local scale. Now let's look at habitat on a more global scale. *Biomes* are these large geographical areas characterized by things like climate, weather, plant life (a.k.a. *flora*), and animal life (a.k.a. *fauna*). Note the following examples:

Tundra—Way, way up north. Few, if any, trees. One layer of the soil is permanently frozen (called *permafrost*). There's a short growing season here. Mostly grasses and wildflowers grow in this region. Animal life includes lemmings, arctic foxes, snowy owls, caribou, and reindeer.

Taiga—Northern forest of conifers. Trees are twisted from the wind and stunted. Winters are real cold and real long. Animal life includes caribou, wolves, moose, bear, rabbits, and lynx.

Temperate deciduous forest—Northeast and middle eastern U.S., for example. Trees drop their leaves in winter. Decent amount of precipitation (like rain and snow), warm summer, cold winter. Animal life includes deer, wolves, bear, small mammals, birds.

Grasslands—The Midwest of the U.S. is one place you'll find grassland. Grasses (no surprise) grow here. Summers are hot, winters are cold, rainfall is hard to predict. Animal life includes the prairie dog, bison, foxes, ferrets, grouse, snakes, and lizards.

Deserts—Dry. Arid. Hardly any rainfall. Hardly any plant life here, either. (Cacti come to mind.) Big temperature shifts on any given day—way hot, and then way cold. Animal life includes jack-rabbits (in North America), owls, kangaroo rats, lizards, snakes, tortoises.

Tropical rain forests—Like in South America. Filled with a truly diverse number of plant forms. Lots of rain, and lots of heat. While plant life is luxuriant, soil quality is poor. Animal life is exotic, abundant, varied: sloths, snakes, monkeys, brilliantly colored birds, leopards, and insects, insects, insects.

CHECK YOUR PROGRESS 5

1. Which biome is associated with soil labeled permafrost? _____

2. Which biome receives so little rainfall that few plants can actually exist there?

3. Which biome contains the most varied plant forms?
   _____

4. You're wandering through the vegetation and the bare branches of the trees allow you to glimpse a deer and a bear (not together) during your trek. What biome are you most likely in?
   A. Grassland
   B. Tundra
   C. Taiga
   D. Temperate deciduous forest

5. You started out on this day hike with a flimsy shirt, which felt just right at the time. Now you feel like you're freezing to death. What's more, your water's running low and this land is dry as bones. You're ready to arm-wrestle a passing jack-rabbit to find a source of water around here. What biome are you in?
   A. Tropical rain forest
   B. Tundra
   C. Desert
   D. Grassland

6. Good thing you packed all that long underwear, because it's freezing here. The wind is unbelievable; you're beginning to feel as bent over as all the stubby evergreens surrounding you. What's really got you preoccupied, though, is the way that lynx keeps circling back to you. What biome are you in?

   A. Tundra
   B. Taiga
   C. Tropical rain forest
   D. Temperate deciduous forest

7. You are beyond soaked and beyond drenched. A new word needs to be invented that can do justice to how wet you really are. It's all that humidity in the air. You don't have time to dwell on it though, because a large anaconda is easing toward you from the upper stories of the forest. What biome are you in?

   A. Tropical rain forest
   B. Desert
   C. Grassland
   D. Taiga

8. In every direction you look, there seems to be no end to the horizon. Where are all the trees around here? You didn't realize you had a fear of open spaces until you ended up in this place. The wildflowers are a nice distractor, though. You're the largest thing around—that is, until a thundering herd of caribou head your way. What biome are you in?

   A. Taiga
   B. Tundra
   C. Grassland
   D. Desert

GLOSSARY

biome
> a large geographical region characterized by climate, temperature, precipitation, flora and fauna

carnivore
> meat-eater

climax community
> the final, most stable and diverse plant community to inhabit a site in an ecological succession

commensalism
> a form of symbiosis; a partnership in which one member benefits and the other is neither helped nor harmed

conifers
> evergreen trees; they hold on to their leaves in the winter; leaves are modified into spikes to withstand cold; examples are pine, cedar, balsam, fir

consumers
> heterotrophs; organisms that must eat others in order to obtain nutrition

deciduous trees
> trees that lose their leaves in the winter; examples are oak, hickory, beech, maple

decomposers
> organisms that free up basic materials—like minerals, carbon dioxide, and water—from dead organisms

evolution
> a change in the genetic make-up of a population over many generations

fauna
> animal life

fitness
> a measure of how well an animal is able to compete for limited resources

flora
> plant life

herbivore
> plant-eater

lichen
> a pioneer organism; product of a symbiotic association of algae and fungi

mutualism
> a form of symbiosis; a partnership in which both members benefit

niche
>a concept that takes into account an animal's entire lifestyle, such as habitat, food source, forage habits, mating season, etc.

nitrogen-fixing bacteria
>important source of nitrogen supply to plants; these bacteria enter into a symbiotic relationship with plants bearing root nodules (i.e., pea plants and clover)

omnivore
>eats meat and plants

parasitism
>a form of symbiosis; a parasite enters into a symbiotic relationship and benefits at the expense of its partner

permafrost
>a permanently frozen layer of soil in the tundra

pioneer community
>the first plant forms to colonize a site in an ecological succession

population
>a group of organisms within a species that share the same habitat

producers
>i.e., plants, blue-green algae; organisms that photosynthesize, producing their own food source

saprophytes
>decomposers; these heterotrophs get their nutrition from dead organisms; examples include fungi (such as mushrooms) and some bacteria

species
>a group of organisms with enough genes in common to successfully interbreed

succession
>an ecological term; encompasses a sequence of plant forms that inhabit a site over time, from pioneer to climax community

symbiosis
>when two organisms of different species live together

taiga
>a biome characterized by stunted, windswept trees and long, cold winters

tundra
>a biome characterized by few if any trees, a layer of permafrost soil; supports grasses and wildflowers in summer

ANSWER KEY

Check Your Progress 1

1. D
2. B
3. A
4. C
5. B
6. D
7. minerals, carbon dioxide, water
8. A

Check Your Progress 2

1. D
2. C
3. B
4. D
5. A
6. A

Check Your Progress 3

1. D
2. II
3. II
4. I
5. D
6. commensalism

Check Your Progress 4

1. pioneer community

2. climax community

3. A

4. A

5.

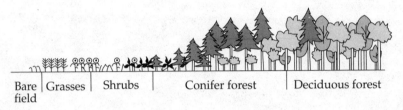

Bare field | Grasses | Shrubs | Conifer forest | Deciduous forest

6. C

Check Your Progress 5

1. tundra

2. desert

3. tropical rain forest

4. D

5. C

6. B

7. A

8. B

NOTES

NOTES

NOTES

About the Author

Deborah Guest holds a bachelor of science degree from Columbia University. She spent two years as a teaching assistant in the Biological Sciences at Columbia University, was a research assistant at the Psychiatric Institute of New York, where she worked with SAD (seasonal affective disorder) patients, and an associate editor at Genetic Engineering News. She has worked for the Princeton Review as a writer, editor, and private tutor since 1989. She is currently a freelance writer and editor specializing in medicine and biology.